Sessions *with*

Luke

Following Jesus on the *Journey* to *Christian Character*

Timothy W. Brock

SMYTH&HELWYS
PUBLISHING, INCORPORATED — MACON, GEORGIA

Acknowledgements

This series of lessons was based on A Lenten Bible Study for
The Thursday Morning Bible Study at the Fredericksburg Baptist
Church, Fredericksburg, Virginia (1989-1998).

This book is dedicated in honor and in memory of the remarkable
Virginia Baptist women involved in that study.

Smyth & Helwys Publishing, Inc.
6316 Peake Road
Macon, Georgia 31210-3960
1-800-747-3016
© 2005 by Smyth & Helwys Publishing
All rights reserved.
Printed in the United States of America.

The paper used in this publication meets the minimum
requirements of American National Standard for Information
Sciences—Permanence of Paper for Printed Library Materials.

Library of Congress Cataloging-in-Publication Data

Brock, Timothy W., 1958-
Sessions with Luke : following Jesus on the journey to Christian
character / by Timothy W. Brock.
p. cm.
Includes bibliographical references.
ISBN 1-57312-446-X (pbk. : alk. paper)
1. Bible. N.T. Luke--Study and teaching.
2. Bible. N.T.
Luke--Criticism, interpretation, etc.
I. Title.

BS2596.B76 2005
226.4'0071--dc22

2005013027

Table of Contents

Sessions with Luke

Sessions with Luke is a ten-lesson study unit designed to help participants explore and embody Christian character through reflection on biblical truths illustrated in the book of Luke.

The Gospel According to Luke is a brilliant collection of memorable stories, challenging teachings, and well-known parables describing the life and work of Jesus Christ. Written by "the beloved Physician Luke," the Gospel and its companion work, The Acts of the Apostles, provide "an orderly account" of the ministry of Jesus and the birth of the Church. Luke chronicled stories in which Jesus invited all types of people to "Follow me." Some people accepted this invitation, literally, and joined Jesus as he journeyed through villages, towns, and cities. As they traveled, he taught his followers and ministered to the needs of the crowds. His teachings and his actions challenged conventional religious practices of the day. Jesus ate with notorious sinners, associated with women, and confronted religious leaders. In similar fashion, Jesus challenged conventional religious beliefs. Jesus proclaimed Good News for all people, not only for the Jews. He also announced that God's special blessing belonged to the poor, not to the wealthy. Ultimately, the stories found in the Third Gospel demonstrated that accepting the invitation to follow Jesus required a radically transformed understanding of relationship with God and with other people.

A transformed understanding is, however, only one part of accepting the invitation to follow Jesus. In the Third Gospel, a *transformed* understanding about relationship with God and with others led to a *transforming* relationship with God and others. Jesus' invitation to "Follow me" is a personal challenge to a radically transformed lifestyle. In Luke's account of the Gospel Story, the followers of Jesus are encouraged to emulate and to embody the character of Christ as they created a lifestyle of obedience to God and service to others.

This study is designed to help participants explore the character of Jesus Christ and to embody the radical lifestyle of a disciple of Jesus Christ.

Resource Pages

Each session includes a resource page listing several questions. These questions invite participants in the study to further explore the biblical content associated with each lesson and to make connections between the biblical truths identified in the Gospel and their own life experiences. The resource pages may be used by a seminar leader in preparation for and during the presentation of the lesson. Study participants may also use the questions to prepare for the session.

Introducing the Gospel of Luke

While many important themes are explored in The Gospel According to Luke, the principal emphasis of this study is discipleship developed through the formation of Christian character. In Luke's account of the life and ministry of Jesus, character transformation is central. Through his actions and in his teachings, Jesus modeled and taught his followers what it meant to develop the character of a disciple. Then, he challenged them to *be* disciples, to live a unique lifestyle thoroughly grounded in Christian character, a lifestyle that is often at odds with conventional wisdom and practice.

The writer of the Gospel of Luke described a three-step process of spiritual formation through which Jesus invited his followers to embrace Christian discipleship through character formation. First, in the early days of his ministry, Jesus invited all sorts of people to join him on a journey, a walkabout through the Judean countryside. In this phase of the process, Jesus initiated relationships and modeled discipleship for his followers, focusing on specific qualities of a disciple. In a second phase of the spiritual formation, Jesus motivated for ministry. He taught his followers and commissioned his disciples to demonstrate these character traits as they were sent out to minister to all types of people, often people on the margins of society. In a third phase of spiritual formation, Jesus taught his disciples to manage their lifestyles. He challenged each of his disciples to follow his example by embodying a uniquely Christian character through a lifestyle of ministry and service (Schroeder, 12-13).

Background for the Study

The following background information, based on an historical/critical study of the texts, will be helpful as you prepare to lead or to participate in this study.

Authorship

Traditionally, it has been assumed that both the third Gospel and The Acts of the Apostles were written by the same person, to the same person or group of people (Craddock, 9). The recipient of these materials was identified in both texts as "most excellent Theophilus." However, the name of the author was not included in the texts. By the late second and early third centuries, custodians of the early Christian tradition attributed both works to Luke, a Gentile convert who was a friend and traveling companion of the Apostle Paul. In fact, a late third century prologue to the Gospel described the author:

> Luke was a Syrian of Antioch, a doctor by profession, who was a disciple of apostles, and later followed Paul until his martyrdom. He served the Lord, without distraction, unmarried, childless, and fell asleep at the age of 84 in Boetia, full of the Holy Spirit. (Heard, 11)

Although research pertaining to authorship of these books has been considered inconclusive, most evangelical scholars embraced the tradition that the writer of the third Gospel was "the beloved Physician Luke" (Craddock, 17).

What do we know about Luke? In addition to the information included in the late third century prologue, a number of assumptions about Luke have been made. First, because he was a physician, one can assume that Luke was a working-class man. In first century society, doctors were associated with the lower social classes; he was, perhaps, an artisan or a slave. Second, in spite of his social station, most biblical scholars agree that Luke was well educated, both medically and rhetorically. The vocabulary and grammar used in the Gospel and in Acts indicate that Luke was a skilled writer with an extraordinary command of Greek. Third, Luke was a great storyteller. He possessed a unique ability to develop broad, universal themes while at the same time providing interesting snapshots of common life and practice. Through stories about and teachings of Jesus recorded only in the third Gospel, Luke introduced his readers to some of the most memorable and evocative characters in scripture (Culpepper, 9).

THE WRITING PROCESS

As a friend and traveling companion of Paul, Luke may well have been an active participant in many of the events recorded in The Acts of the Apostles. He was not, however, an eyewitness to the life and ministry of Jesus of Nazareth. Luke had to depend on the testimony of other persons and on other sources of information. In the prologue of the Gospel, Luke 1:1-4, the author provided insights into the process that he used to write "an orderly account" of the life and ministry of Jesus. Luke stated his desire to "compile a narrative, depending on eyewitnesses and ministers of the word."

Who were these eyewitnesses and ministers? To what documents or sources of information did Luke refer as he penned the third Gospel? These questions have been a matter of much speculation in biblical research. In brief, the compilation process used by Luke has been described as follows.

First, biblical scholars believe that, prior to the writing of the four Gospels, a number of documents describing the life and ministry of Jesus were in circulation among first century churches. They further speculate that one of these documents was a specific collection of teachings of Jesus. They called this document Q, or *Quelle*, the German word for "source." Because the Gospels of Matthew and Luke share a common body of information found in no other Gospel, these scholars suspect that both the writer of Matthew and Luke had access to a copy of Q as each wrote. The Sermon on the Mount in Matthew and its parallel, the Sermon on the Plain in Luke, are examples of material that scholars believe to be included in the Q document.

Second, most biblical scholars accept the premise that the Gospel According to Mark was the earliest Gospel, written between AD 65 and AD 72. Further, they believe that by the time Luke compiled his account of the Gospel, the Gospel of Mark had been in circulation among the first century churches for some time. Because a significant number of the verses in the Gospel of Mark are also included, with little variation, in the Gospels of Matthew and Luke, it is assumed that both Matthew and Luke had access to a copy of the Gospel of Mark as they wrote. The feeding of the five thousand is one example of a pericope, or a portion of the Gospel story, included with little variation in all three of these Gospels.

Finally, approximately twenty-five percent of stories, teachings, and parables found in Luke's account are found in no other Gospel (7). For example, a number of stories associated with the birth of Jesus, that is, the infancy narratives, Luke 1:5–2:52, are found only in the third Gospel. These narratives include stories about members of the holy family: Zechariah's epiphany in the Temple, Elizabeth's unexpected pregnancy, the birth of John the Baptist, Mary's response to the news of her untimely pregnancy, and the dedication of Jesus in the Temple. Further, the parable of the Prodigal Son and the parable of the Unjust Steward are two examples of material found only in the third Gospel.[7]

Scholars believed that Luke alone had access to one or more separate collections of documents in which these unique stories, parables, and teachings were recorded. Further, the fact that Luke included the personal testimonies of members of Jesus' family led a small number of scholars to speculate that he may have had access to a private collection of documents from members of the holy family. Some of these stories may have been delivered, directly or indirectly, from Mary, the Mother of Jesus.[8]

If this theory does indeed reflect Luke's writing process, then the following table provides an overview of the sources used to produce the Gospel of Luke (Wright, 87):

• Luke 1:1–2:52 Material unique to Luke
• Luke 3:1–6:19 Materials derived from the Gospel of Mark and *Q*
• Luke 6:20–8:3 Materials derived from *Q* and unique to Luke
• Luke 8:4–9:50 Materials derived from the Gospel of Mark
• Luke 9:51–18:14 Materials derived from *Q* and unique to Luke
• Luke 18:15–24:11 Materials derived from Mark and unique to Luke
• Luke 24:12-53 Material unique to Luke

DATE OF WRITING

Based on the assumptions about the writing process previously described, biblical scholars speculate that the Gospel According to Luke was written in the last third of the first century (Craddock, 18). More specifically, Luke probably wrote the Gospel between AD 80 and AD 85 (Culpepper, 7).

AUDIENCE

Again, it has been assumed that both the third Gospel and The Acts of the Apostles were written to the same person or group of persons. The recipient identified in both texts was "most excellent Theophilus." Some scholars believed that this phrase referred to a specific individual, probably a Roman of high rank and social status. Others believed that the Gospel was written, not to a specific person, but to a group of persons who were "lovers of God," the literal translation of the name. In this view, the audience was a group of first-century God-fearers, Hellenists who had been attracted to Judaism, to the God of Israel, and to the worship in the synagogue. As spiritually-sensitive people, these God-fearers were intrigued by the stories and beliefs of the developing Christian tradition (Craddock, 15-16).

Whether originally intended for an individual or for a group, many biblical scholars affirm the long-standing traditional assumption that Luke, as a Gentile Christian, wrote his Gospel for the Gentile church of the late first century. These scholars viewed the Gospel as a pastoral document concerned with issues within a church that was moving increasingly beyond its Jewish foundations and traditions. This position can be supported by a careful reading of the Gospel. Scholars agree that, for a Gentile, Luke had a remarkable knowledge of the Jewish scriptures; he did not, however, attempt to prove that Jesus was the fulfillment of the Old Testament prophecies, as was the case with the writer of the Gospel of Matthew. Instead, Luke emphasized the universal scope of Jesus' ministry as Savior of not just the Jews, but of all humankind. This emphasis would indeed have been good news for spiritually-sensitive, first century Gentiles, and Luke would have been an ideal person to convey this message to this audience (Tolbert, 8-9).

THEMES

As a master storyteller, Luke possessed the unique ability to reflect on common experience in order to develop universal, theological themes. In *The New Interpreter's Bible Commentary*, Baptist scholar Alan Culpepper identifies six interrelated themes developed in the Gospel of Luke (Culpepper, 20-30).

God's Redemptive Purposes. Luke provided both an accurate record of the life of Jesus in its historical context and a theological reflection on that context. The primary purpose of this theological reflection was to emphasize that all the events and teaching recorded in the Gospel were ultimately a part of God's redemptive plan for the salvation of all humanity.

Salvation for All. In sharing the stories, parables, and teachings of Jesus, Luke communicated the radical message that Jesus announced salvation for all people, regardless of their religious background or social standing. Luke celebrated the radical inclusiveness of Jesus' ministry with all types of people—sinners, Samaritans, tax collectors, women, and social outcasts.

The Blessings of Poverty and the Dangers of Wealth. The previous theme was amplified in the manner in which Luke portrayed poor people. At a time when popular theology held that the rich were blessed by God, Luke recorded stories in which Jesus taught that God would lift up the poor and cast out the rich.

Table Fellowship. Luke filled his Gospel with meal scenes; Jesus was either going to a meal, at a meal, or coming from a meal. In Luke, hospitality and table fellowship created a unique opportunity for community. Jesus chose to share meals with all types of people: with his disciples and with the crowds, with the scribes and the Pharisees, and with tax collectors and sinners. While "at table," Jesus taught and ministered to people. For Luke, the Gospel was most effectively embodied at the dinner table. (26-27)

The Role of a Disciple. In the Gospel According to Luke, the role of a disciple was best summarized by an unconditional, absolute, person-centered call from Jesus: "Follow me." In this book, Jesus offered himself as the model for all humanity, a model to imitated in attitude, action, and character. Jesus lived a life that reflected the character of obedience to God. The disciple must be obedient. Jesus lived a life empowered by the Spirit. The disciple must be dependent on the power of God. His life was driven by his understanding of his personhood and his mission in life. The disciples must also understand their personhood and purpose. Because he understood who he was and to what he had been called, Jesus was compassionate toward the poor and oppressed. He healed and forgave all types of people. Compassion, healing, and forgiveness must also characterize the disciples of Jesus. He demonstrated spiritual discipline as he regularly withdrew to quiet, desolate places to pray. The disciple must be disciplined and spiritually sensitive. Jesus suffered the consequences of living out his mission and died a model martyr's death. The disciple must be willing to lose life in order to find life. As he modeled, motivated, and managed his life, Jesus showed his followers that discipleship had radical implications.

The Importance of an Accurate Witness. As previously indicated, Luke was not an eyewitness to the events about which he wrote. A compelling concern for an accurate and continuing witness guided Luke in writing the Gospel, "So that you may know the truth concerning the things about which you have been instructed." (Lk 1:4, NRSV)

GENERAL OUTLINE
The following outline provides a listing of the major sections of the Gospel According to Luke (10):

• Luke 1:1-4 The Prologue
• Luke 1:5–2:52 The Infancy Narratives
• Luke 3:1–4:13 Preparation for the Ministry of Jesus
• Luke 4:14–9:50 The Ministry in Galilee
• Luke 9:51–19:27 The Journey to Jerusalem
• Luke 19:28–21:38 The Ministry in Jerusalem
• Luke 22:1–24:53 The Passion and Resurrection Narratives

Summary

The Gospel According to Luke tells the story of how Jesus' original followers were invited to participate in the journey of discipleship, moving from modeling character, to motivating for ministry, and finally to managing lifestyle. As you participate in this study of the book of Luke, you are invited to follow Jesus on the same journey of discipleship through the formation of Christian character.

Introducing the Gospel of Luke

Character Formed in a Faithful Family

Session 1   *Focal Passages: Luke1:5-25, 1:26-38, 1:46-56, and 2:41-52*

Central Truth of the Session

Personal character is first formed in the context of family. As an infant and as a child, Jesus of Nazareth was raised in a family of dedicated and spiritually-sensitive women and men. In the face of the unusual circumstances that surrounded his birth, these relatives demonstrated faith in God and in God's purposes. By their actions, these people embodied faithfulness and passed that trait on to Jesus.

Parenting as an Act of Faith

In the best of circumstances, birthing and rearing children is an act of faith: faith in parents and family members, faith in the future, and ultimately, faith in God. As a mother and father gaze at the face of their child sleeping in the cradle, they become aware that this newborn offers the opportunity to redeem the past and to impart cherished hopes and dreams to the next generation. With patience and maturity, the nurture, care, comfort, and protection of a child can become a spiritual discipline, a discipline that can build and form the character of both parent and child. During the childhood years, it is the responsibility of parents and family members to hand children a heritage. Then, as they mature and gain experience, children can provide parents with new awareness, perception, and insight. In time, if they are open to their children's questions, parents may be challenged anew about life and its varied meanings. The questions of the older child confront parents with their own unanswered and unarticulated issues and dreams (Nelson, 492-93).

In light of the highly unusual circumstances surrounding his conception, the birthing and rearing of Jesus of Nazareth was indeed a profound act of faith. A young woman and various members of her family were asked to demonstrate a remarkable level of faith in themselves, in the future of all humanity, and ultimately, in God when she became pregnant prior to her marriage. In faith, as this mother gazed at her child in the manger, her personal hopes and dreams for her son were tempered by her knowledge that this child would indeed redeem the past and communicate God's vision for the future. This child's character would develop in a faithful home. From his parents and other members of his family, this child would learn about his rich family and religious heritage. Eventually, this child would grow and mature to the point that he would ask deep questions, questions that cause religious leaders, and even his mother, to reflect on life and faith in fresh ways.

Setting the Context

The focal passages for this lesson were selected from the infancy narratives, Luke 1:5–2:52. As indicated in the introduction to the study, the stories contained in this section of scripture are found only in the Gospel of Luke. These verses provide the reader of the Gospel with a unique perspective regarding a number of events surrounding the birth of Jesus, a selected event from his childhood, and his family's reactions to all of these events.

Biblical scholars have developed a number of insights regarding the interpretation of these passages. First, scholars have noted the highly personal nature of the stories included in this section of the book. In these passages, intimate images and reflections of members of the holy family were shared in detail. Because of the highly personal content of these stories, some scholars have speculated that Mary or other members of the holy family may have recorded their own stories in a collection of private documents. According to this theory, Luke alone had access to these family diaries as he wrote his Gospel (Culpepper, 7). Second, some scholars speculate that Luke felt compelled to include these unique stories in order to address lingering questions about the circumstances surrounding Jesus' birth, especially with regard to the virgin conception. Third, other scholars believe that The Infancy Narrative were not included in the earliest versions of the Gospel. These experts speculate that someone other than Luke, again to address specific challenges to Jesus' parentage, added this section later. If these scholars are correct, the Gospel, as Luke wrote it, actually began with Luke 3:1, with both John and Jesus as adults (Craddock, 21).

Regardless of the source of the material or the timing of their writing, these passages provide the reader with unique insights into the family in which Jesus grew up, was nurtured, and first experienced faith.

A Faithful Extended Family

The infancy narratives begin with a remarkable story about members of Jesus' extended family. In Luke 1:5-25, the reader of the Gospel was introduced to Zechariah, a priest of the order of Abijah, and Elizabeth, his wife. Elizabeth, who was also descended from the priestly line of Aaron, was described as a relative, though not necessarily a cousin, of Mary (See Lk 1:36). The couple lived in a Judean town in the hill country (See Lk 1:39). The scriptures described Zechariah and Elizabeth as a pious couple, righteous before God and living blamelessly according to the Law. Their piety, however, was juxtaposed against their childlessness. Like Abraham and Sarah before them, the couple was advanced in age and had no child. In that context, it was assumed that the wife was responsible for the failure to have children; the scriptures concurred with that assessment. Further, barrenness was regarded, at best, a social stigma and, at worst, a sign of God's punishment. The scriptures implied that the couple lived in the tension between personal piety and public disgrace (Culpepper, 45) (See Lk 1:25).

As a descendent of the priestly class, Zechariah was a member of one of twenty-four divisions of priests. Twice annually, and for a period of one week each time, the members of each division were required to travel to Jerusalem to serve in the Temple. The priests performed a variety of tasks associated with public worship. Their most important task was performing sacrifices on two main altars in the Temple complex. One of these altars was located in a courtyard outside the sanctuary. In this public venue, the people could watch the priest as he led in worship. A second altar was located inside the sanctuary, out of public view. Twice each day, while the people prayed, sacrifices were offered and incense was burned simultaneously on these two altars. The priests would typically draw lots to determine which of the two altars each would serve. It was considered a high honor to be selected to serve the inner altar (45-46).

On one occasion, Zechariah was chosen to perform the sacrifices and burn the incense on the altar in the inner sanctuary. In that high and holy place, while performing a sacred function, Zechariah encountered the angel Gabriel, a messenger sent from the presence of God. Not surprisingly, Zechariah was overwhelmed and fearful. Gabriel offered words of comfort, words of promise, and words of mild rebuke to the frightened priest. The words of comfort were, "Do not be afraid for your prayers have been answered" (See Lk 1:11). The words of promise came in four parts:

• You and your wife will have a son whom you will name John.
• The birth of this child will bring great joy and gladness to you, your wife, and to many others because he will be favored by God.
• You will raise your son according to the Nazirite vows. (See Numbers 6:3 and Judges 13:2-5.)
• Your son will speak with a prophetic voice like Elijah and will prepare the people for the coming of the Lord (Craddock, 26).

The mild rebuke came when Zechariah questioned the words of promise. Even a pious and faithful man such as Zechariah found it hard to believe that he and Elizabeth could have a child. When he questioned the prophecy, Gabriel informed him that he would unable to speak until the day that the prophecy was fulfilled, i.e., the birth of the child.

Outside, in the courtyard of the Temple, the people were waiting for Zechariah to emerge from the inner sanctum and to pronounce a blessing. When he finally came out, he was unable to speak. Crude sign language was inadequate to communicate what had happened. The people concluded, correctly, that he must have experienced some form of vision while in the inner sanctuary. Awed by his encounter and still unable to speak, the dutiful priest completed his tour of duty and returned home.

In spite of his initial skepticism, Zechariah and Elizabeth conceived a child. It was then time for Elizabeth to be overwhelmed by the good news of the impending birth. She secluded herself from the community, from the same people who had viewed her with disgrace. Instead of proclaiming the news from the rooftops, she chose to privately reflect on her great fortunes. Zechariah was mute, but obedient. Elizabeth was pregnant and cloistered. Both members of Jesus' extended family were faithful in unbelievable circumstance. Their faith culminated in the birth of their son, John. (See Lk 1:57-80)

A Risky Faithfulness

In The Annunciation of the Birth of Jesus, Luke 1:26-38, the Gospel writer recorded a second story of faith in the context of unbelievable circumstances. In some ways, the situation described in this second narrative was similar to the situation outlined in the first story:

Zechariah and Elizabeth were both described as pious and righteous people. The same description applied to Mary. In various verses in the infancy narratives, Mary was described as "thoughtful" (1:29), "favored by God" and obedient (1:30), believing and worshipful (1:46-55), and devoted to Jewish law and piety (2:22-51) (27–28).

In his encounter with Gabriel, Zechariah received a four-part promise. In her encounter with Gabriel, Mary received a series of promises. First, the angel told her that she would have a son and that his name would be Jesus. Second, he promised that the child would be called "The Son of the Most High" and that he would reign on the throne of his ancestor (by adoption), David. Third, the angel assured Mary that she would conceive through the power of the Holy Spirit and that, because of this unique conception, the child would be holy. And fourth, the angel offered Elizabeth's pregnancy as a sign of God's ability to follow through with these promises (28).

In some ways, the situation described in this second story was very different from the dynamics in the first story:

In the first story, the stigma of barrenness was removed as a pious, married couple was finally able to conceive. The resulting birth led to celebration in the community and speculation about the mission the child, John. In the second story, the stigma of pregnancy outside of marriage hung over the head of an engaged teenager. The resulting birth occurred in obscurity, but with heavenly celebrations.

In the first story, a righteous priest encountered an angel in a holy place—the inner sanctuary of the Temple in Jerusalem—while performing a religious ritual, with many witnesses waiting outside. Zechariah would have been a logical recipient of an angelic visitation. In the second story, a righteous peasant girl encountered an angel in an ordinary place—the backwater town of Nazareth—under ordinary circumstances, with no witnesses. Mary was a most unlikely candidate to be used by God for such an important task.

In the first story, the righteous priest questioned the good news spoken by the angel, received a mild rebuke, and experienced the loss of voice. In the second story, the peasant girl accepted the challenge without reservation, in spite of the possible consequences of being pregnant before marriage. (Refer to Deut 22:13-29 for a detailed explanation of the consequences of sexual activity outside the context of marriage.)

Seeking Support from Extended Family

While Zechariah lost his voice as a result of his momentary lack of faith, Mary found a unique voice when she readily accepted God's calling for her life. She used this voice to sing a song of praise, a song recorded in Luke 1:46-55.

Mary's song was recorded in the context of a broader passage of scripture entitled The Visitation, Luke 1:39-56. In this passage, the Gospel writer reported that, after the announcement of the birth of Jesus, Mary left Nazareth to visit Elizabeth in the Judean hill country (See Lk 39-41a.) Some biblical scholars speculated that Mary initiated this visit in order to ascertain the validity of the angel's prophecy about Elizabeth. According to this approach, the only way to see if Elizabeth was indeed pregnant was for Mary to make a visit to her relative. Commentator Fred Craddock discounts this theory. He believes that Mary had already accepted Gabriel's word as gospel truth. Craddock believed that Mary was drawn to Elizabeth by a common experience and for mutual support. It was simply a case of one family member needing the company of another (29).

When Mary arrived at the home of Zechariah and Elizabeth, she offered words of greeting to her hostess. Verses 41b-45 record an "inspired speech" delivered by Elizabeth upon hearing this greeting. A spiritually-sensitive person, Elizabeth was overwhelmed by Mary's presence. Filled with the Holy Spirit, Elizabeth praised both Mary and her unborn child. She blessed Mary on two grounds. First, Elizabeth exalted Mary because she had been chosen to the mother of the Lord. Second, Elizabeth affirmed Mary because she had immediately believed the promise of God and had responded in humility to the responsibility.

Mary's response to this outpouring of the Spirit was to give voice to her own feelings in song. Traditionally, this song, recorded in Luke 1:46-55, has been identified as The Magnificant, so termed from the opening word in the Latin translation. (Note: Some scholars have speculated that this passage was heavily influenced by the prayer of Hannah found in 1 Samuel 2:1-10 [Tolbert, 24].) The first section of the passage is autobiographical. In verses 46-49, Mary offered personal words of praise to God for the special favor that God bestowed on her, even though she was a handmaiden of low estate. The remainder of the passage expanded these words of personal testimony to demonstrate a general principle about the nature of God and the pattern of God's relationship with humanity. Verses 50-55 developed the idea that God's selection of Mary anticipated and modeled what God would do for the poor, the powerless, and the oppressed of the world. In these verses, Mary extolled the God who will bring down the mighty and will exalt those of low degree, the God who will fill the hungry and will send the rich away empty. In the final analysis, the unexpected choice of Mary to fulfill this unique role in God's plan mirrored the complete reversal of fortunes that will characterize the ultimate fulfillment of God's promises to Israel and to all humanity.

In Luke 1:56, the Visitation story ended with a simple statement. Mary stayed with Elizabeth for three months, presumably through the birth of John, and then returned to own home (Craddock, 29-31).

Faithfulness Embodied in the Child of a Dedicated Family

The story of Jesus in the temple, Luke 2:41-52, is the only Gospel account of a childhood experience in the life of Jesus.

Why tell did Luke choose to include this story in his Gospel? Biblical scholars speculated that, in both The Dedication of Jesus in the Temple (Lk 2:21-38) and in this passage, Luke attempted to establish two facts: first, that Jesus' family actively and faithfully practiced the Jewish faith, and second, that, from birth, Jesus was thoroughly grounded in the heritage and rituals of Judaism (41). In sharing the dedication stories, Luke demonstrated that Joseph and Mary followed the rituals associated with the birth of a first-born, male child. (See Leviticus 12:2-8.) In relating the Story of Jesus in the Temple, Luke reported the fact that the family made annual pilgrimages to Jerusalem for religious festivals. As outlined in Exodus 23:14-17, all male Israelites, and by implications, their families, should travel each year to Jerusalem to celebrate the festivals of Passover, Pentecost, and Tabernacles. If the family lived at some distance from Jerusalem, all efforts should be made to celebrate at least Passover in Jerusalem. In the end, the passages conveyed the impression that, as good, Jewish parents, Joseph and Mary both practiced the faith and modeled the faith for their son.

This passage described the annual pilgrimage to Jerusalem for the Passover Festival during the year that Jesus was twelve years old. At age twelve, it was unlikely that Jesus had yet participated in the Jewish rituals signaling the transition from childhood to adulthood. But as an older child, Jesus would have been given some measure of independence both during their journey to and from Jerusalem and during their stay in the city. While in Jerusalem, Jesus may have been allowed to explore the city with friends and relatives, checking in with his parents on occasion. At the conclusion of the festival, Joseph and Mary began their trip back home, assuming that Jesus was somewhere in the group of travelers. Moving at a pace of fifteen miles a day, their journey from Jerusalem to Nazareth should have taken four or five days (Culpepper, 76). Their journey was cut short when they discovered that Jesus was not in the caravan.

The anxious parents retraced their steps up the steep hill that led to the city. For three fear-filled days, they searched in vain for their wayward child. At last, they discovered their son on the grounds of the Temple complex. In all probability, Jesus had joined a small group of rabbis in one of the side halls adjacent to the outer courts of the complex. Using a Socratic approach to teaching, that is, asking questions, soliciting individual answers, and critiquing the responses, these rabbis and their students would spend hours in spirited debate. As a novice, Jesus would not have played a prominent role of leadership in these discussions, but the scriptures indicated that the rabbis were amazed with his understanding and his responses. For a child raised by a peasant family and educated in a provincial synagogue, Jesus was astonishing (Gilmour, 67).

His behavior also astonished his anxious parents, particularly his mother. The same Mary who had once so readily accepted the words of promise offered by Gabriel so many years before was now a fretting parent who had not seen her son for at least four days! The same Mary who had once sung the praises of God for her role in God's redemption of humanity was now the mother of an inconsiderate child! In a rather terse rebuke, Mary chided Jesus: "Child, why have you treated us like this? Look, your father and I have been searching for you in great anxiety" (Lk 2:48b, NRSV).

The scriptures implied that Jesus is also astonished at his mother's response to the situation. In paraphrase, he said, "You, above all others, should have known where I would be. I now understand what you have known all along; I must be in my Father's house, doing my Father's business." According to Craddock, this passage demonstrates that, at age twelve, Jesus had already claimed for himself a unique relationship to God. To this point, other people had proclaimed and celebrated this relationship: in the angel Gabriel's annunciation to Mary, in Elizabeth's reaction to Mary's visit, and in Simeon's and Anna's reaction to Jesus during his dedication in the Temple (See Lk 2:22-38). Now, in the context of parental anxiety and disappointment, Jesus demonstrated faithfulness to God and to God's purposes as he claimed his own unique relationship to God and his special responsibilities (Craddock, 42).

The scriptures stated that Joseph and Mary did not understand their son's response or reaction to their concerns. Nonetheless, Jesus returned home with his family while Mary "treasured all these things in her heart" (Lk 2:51, NRSV). As Jesus continued to grow and mature in the context of his dedicated peasant family, he demonstrated the faithfulness that he had seen embodied in his parents and member of his family. God and others smiled on the person that he was becoming. In his response to his parents in the Temple and in the process of becoming the man that God had called him to be, Jesus demonstrated an important truth: family love and loyalties have their place and flourish when the higher love and loyalty go to God (42-43).

Summary of the Session

The environment created in the home, the values espoused there, and the behaviors exhibited in everyday living set the stage for the faith development of children. The focal passages selected for this lesson explored how family faithfulness, even in the face of unbelievable circumstances and risky consequences, helped to shape the character of Jesus as a child.

Resource Page

Based on your reading of the lesson's focal passages and background material, write a definition of the term "faithfulness."

_____

_____

_____

_____

_____

_____

How did Zechariah and Elizabeth each embody and model faithfulness to God's calling?

_____

_____

_____

_____

_____

_____

How did Mary embody and model faithfulness to God's calling?

_____

_____

_____

_____

_____

_____

Reflecting on your own experience, identify one or two members of your extended family or your church family who have embodied and modeled faithfulness to God's calling for you. Describe that person or persons. Then describe in as much detail as possible how their faithfulness has impacted your life and character.

_____

_____

_____

_____

_____

2 Character Grounded in Identity

Focal Passages: Luke 3:21-22, 3:23-38,
and 4:1-15

Central Truth of the Lesson

In a time filled with messianic expectations, Jesus began his public ministry with a clear understanding of his own identity and his unique relationship with God. When faced with the temptation to misinterpret his identity or misuse his authority, Jesus remained faithful to God. Following his example, contemporary disciples of Jesus should develop an authentic understanding of personal identity, strive for an intimate relationship with God, and resist the temptation to be less than or other than what we are called to be in Christ.

Setting the Context: Transcending the Time

Uncertainty and expectation. These two words could easily be used to describe first-century Palestine, the context for the life and ministry of Jesus of Nazareth. Israel, the once proud and independent Kingdom of David and Solomon, was now an insignificant and occupied country. Officials of the Roman government and their well-trained armies enforced *Pax Roma*, the peace of Rome, with brutal efficiency. The people of Israel were required to pay taxes to the Roman emperors, to perform services for their Roman occupiers, and to bargain with their Roman overlords for the right to participate in their own religious practices.

How did the people of Israel respond to this occupation? Some individuals and groups, such as the tax collectors, collaborated with their occupiers in order to prosper under difficult circumstances. Other groups, such as the Zealots and various insurrectionist parties, actively rebelled against Roman authority, participating in guerilla warfare. Still other Jewish people faced the occupation with renewed religious fervor. In times of instability, people often turn or return to the scrupulous practice of their faith. In first century Palestine, prophetic preachers such as John the Baptist drew large crowds of ordinary people seeking both comfort and challenge in this time of trouble. The religious establishment—the leaders of the synagogues, the scribes, and the priests in Jerusalem—and the various sects of Judaism—the Sadducees, the Pharisees, and the Essenes—also struggled with the question of how to remain faithful to the tenets of the faith while living under pagan occupation. Each of these groups developed its own responses to this dilemma.

In spite of the anxieties and frustrations caused by the Roman occupation, or perhaps because of it, first-century Palestine was also a time that was pregnant with messianic expectations. The Jewish people found comfort and hope in the fact that their scriptures promised the coming of a Messiah, a descendent of King David who would restore Israel to her former glory. In the face of occupation, many of the religious leaders and the people anticipated a messiah who would function as a military leader, a powerful general who would repel the armies of occupation and establish a glorious new theocracy in Jerusalem. A few others understood a different role for messiah. In the prophetic literature, this minority discovered a suffering servant, a person who would lead by acts of self-sacrifice, humility, and compassion. Regardless of the understanding of the function, the people of first-century Palestine eagerly awaited the coming of the Messiah.

This particular time and place would be the context in which Jesus of Nazareth would live and minister. As a first-century Palestinian Jew, Jesus was a man of his time. He experienced first-hand both the anxieties of the occupation and excitements of the messianic expectations of the day. But Jesus was also a man who transcended his time; he was not shaped by his context. Instead, he made a series of proactive choices that would ultimately define his mission in life and often put himself at odds with the expectations of his context. Jesus came to a clear understanding of his own identity and of his unique relationship to God. At his baptism, God affirmed this understanding. Then, as demonstrated in his temptations in the desert, Jesus actively resisted enticements to be someone other than God had intended. This sequence of events, recorded in Luke 3:21–4:13 serves as the focus of this session.

The Baptism of Jesus: Ordination for a Mission

Luke's account of the baptism of Jesus is recorded in Luke 3:21-22. This event was considered such an important part of Jesus' personal story that all four Gospel writers included a version of it in their record of his life and ministry (See Mt 3:13-17, Mk 1:9-11, and Jn 1:29-34 for comparison). While the same event was chronicled in each of the four Gospels, there are significant differences in the four accounts.

In the Gospels of Mark and Matthew, the Jordan River was identified as the site of the baptism. Neither Luke nor John indicated a location (Craddock, 50).

In the Gospels of Mark, Matthew, and John, the person who baptized Jesus was clearly identified as John the Baptist. In fact, both Matthew and John indicated that the two had extended conversations around the event of his baptism. These stories stand in stark contrast to Luke's account. Based on Luke 3:19-20, the reader must assume that John was already in prison at the time of Jesus' baptism. Here, the identity of the person who baptized Jesus was not stated (Culpepper, 87).

In each of the four Gospels, Jesus experienced both a manifestation of the Spirit and words of affirmation from heaven. In the Gospels of Mark and Matthew, this experience occurred immediately following the act of baptism, in the presence of many people. In the Gospel of John, John the Baptist alone witnessed this experience, presumably in some other context, and shared his description of the experience with the assembled crowd. In his account of the story, Luke indicated that the manifestation of the Spirit and the words of affirmation occurred after the baptism, while Jesus was engaged in a time of prayer (See Lk 3:21). Luke does not indicate whether Jesus was praying publicly or, as was often the case, praying alone (Craddock, 52).

In the exegesis of the Gospels, when the same event is described in significantly difference ways, biblical scholars assume that each writer was attempting to highlight a different issue or address a different question associated with that story. For example, scholars believe that, in his account of this story, Matthew attempted to explain why Jesus, as a righteous and sinless person, needed to be baptized. The dialogue between John and Jesus prior to the baptism provided one answer to this question (Tolbert, 39). In similar fashion, Luke chose to de-emphasize the act of baptism and to highlight what happened after the event. For Luke, the most crucial aspect of the story was the fact that, while Jesus was in prayer, his understanding of his identify was acknowledged through a special manifestation of the Spirit (as a dove, in bodily form) and through words of affirmation from heaven. For Luke, it was not as important for his reader to know where or by whom Jesus was baptized; it was important for Jesus to know, beyond a shadow of doubt, the nature of his identity and of his relationship with God (Craddock, 51).

Finally, biblical scholars reason that the exact wording this blessing from heaven provided a clue to Jesus' understanding of his mission in life. In Luke 3:22b, a voice from heaven said, "You are My Son, the Beloved; with you I am well pleased." Baptist scholar Malcolm Tolbert noted that these words call to mind the text of Isaiah 42:1, the opening verse of one of the four Servant Poems found in the book of Isaiah. (These poems are found in Isaiah 42:1-4, 49:1-6, 50:4-11, 52:13–53:12.) Tolbert speculated that Jesus recognized an intentional connection between these words of affirmation and that text in Isaiah. This recognition was, according to Tolbert, an indication to Jesus that he would live out his mission in life, not as a military messiah, but as a suffering servant. Based on this interpretation, Tolbert expressed the view that, for Luke, the baptism of Jesus was actually an ordination for a ministry of service and sacrifice (Tolbert, 40).

The Ancestors of Jesus: Back to the Beginning

Sandwiched between Luke's accounts of his baptism and his temptation in the wilderness is a listing of Jesus' ancestors. This genealogy is found in Luke 3:23-38, with a parallel passage located in Matthew 1:1-17. Again, a careful reading of both texts reveals a number of similarities and differences.

The two authors included their genealogies at different positions in their Gospels. Matthew began his account with the listing of ancestors. Luke, however, placed the genealogy in the body of his work, near the beginning of Jesus' public ministry.

In both versions of the genealogy, Jesus' heritage was traced back through the line of Joseph, even though subsequent texts made it very clear that Joseph was not Jesus' biological father. As the adopted son of Joseph, Jesus could claim a legal connection Joseph's ancestors, and thus to King David. This relationship to David would be a critical link to the messianic line (Craddock, 52).

The two texts do not include the same lists of ancestors. While both confirm the fact that Jesus was a "son of David," Luke's list traced Jesus' connection to David through his son, Nathan, while Matthew's list connected Jesus to David through the royal line of King Solomon (Tolbert, 41).

The most significant difference in the two accounts can be found in number of generations included in the genealogy. While Matthew's genealogy traced the line of Jesus back to Abraham, the Father of the Jewish faith, Luke's version mapped Jesus' lineage past Abraham to the origins of all humanity, to Adam, as the original son of God. Some commentators believe that the inclusion of these additional generations of Jesus reflected Luke's desire to establish the universal nature of Jesus' ministry (Craddock, 53). Others speculate that Luke included the additional information and placed the genealogy at this usual place in the narrative, in order to clearly establish Jesus as the Son of God (Culpepper, 95).

A basic principle of sound biblical interpretation is the fact that individual portions of scripture must be read in the context of surrounding passages. Given the nature of the preceding passage (Jesus' ordination for ministry following his baptism) and the nature of subsequent passages (the temptations and the declaration of mission based on this ordination), one may speculate that Luke included this genealogy, at this position in the text, to establish the unique relationship between Jesus of Nazareth and the Creator God.

Tempted to Be Less or Other Than

Having clearly established the sonship of Jesus in the preceding narratives, Luke next recorded the story of a period of temptation that Jesus faced during and after an extended retreat into the Judean wilderness. This story described how Jesus responded when the devil enticed him to misinterpret his sonship and to misuse his power and authority.

Prior to the temptation (Lk 4:1-13), Jesus experienced a personal and spiritual high point in his life. With words of heavenly blessing still ringing in his ears, he felt compelled by the Spirit to retreat in a desolate place, presumably for an extended period of prayer and fasting. This pattern of retreat would be repeated many times during the years of his public ministry. With regard to the location and duration of this experience, Luke probably intended to elicit images of the forty-year period during which the people of Israel wondered in the desert after the exodus from Egypt. During that time, the people were challenged to look to God alone for guidance and to depend on God alone for their basic needs. The same challenge would be placed before Jesus. In a very vulnerable condition, weakened by hunger, Jesus was tempted by the devil, literally, spiritually, or psychologically, to question his relationship to God and his approach to and motivation for ministry.

The first temptation addressed a very practical, physical need: at the end of a forty-day fast, Jesus was "famished" and needed food. In paraphrase, the devil said, "So, you think you are the Son of God. Prove it! Make bread and eat!" This enticement could be understood on several levels. It could be interpreted as a direct challenge to Jesus' understanding of his own identity. In this interpretation, the devil could be seen as attempting to amplify any lingering doubts that Jesus may have had regarding his unique relationship with God. This interpretation of the text, however, is not consistent with previous stories in the third Gospel. According to Luke, by this point in his life, Jesus knew, beyond doubt, his own identity. A different explanation of the text may be more consistent with Luke's purposes. In this approach, the temptations focused, not on the fact of sonship, but more specifically on how Jesus would live out his unique identity. Most probably, the challenge to make bread was a temptation to exploit his sonship for his own benefit or to express his independence from God. Once again, the parallel between the wanderings of the children of Israel and the temptation of Jesus are informative. In the wilderness, the children of Israel were challenged to depend completely on God for their basic needs, including food in the form of manna, a bread-like substance. Here, the devil challenged Jesus to repeat the sign of God's provision for the people. If Jesus had accepted the challenge and made bread for himself, he would have abused his sonship by serving his own needs rather than depending on God's provision for his needs. To that end, in Luke 4:4, Jesus responded to the temptation by quoting the first half of Deuteronomy 8:3: "One does not live by bread alone."

The second temptation dealt with power gained by compromise. In Luke 4:5-8, the devil claimed authority over all the kingdoms of the earth. The devil also claimed the prerogative to transfer that authority to whomever he selected. All he required to affect a transfer of power was a Faustian act of worship. Jesus, however, did not need to sell his soul for authority. In the Gospel of Luke, Jesus, as the Son of God, already possessed ultimate authority, an authority derived from his relationship with God. This authority would serve as the basis of his teaching ministry (refer to Lk 4:32) and his healing ministry (refer to Lk 4:36). Most critically, this relationship gave Jesus the authority to forgive sins (See Lk 5:24). In effect, Jesus already possessed an authority far superior to anything that the devil could offer. So in Luke 4:8, Jesus dismissed the devil's offer by quoting Deuteronomy 6:13: "Worship the Lord your God and serve him only."

The third temptation was a challenge to put God's promises to the test. In a devious twist, the devil even framed this temptation in the form of a scripture quotation, citing Psalm 91:11-12 as a proof text of God's promise of protection. Specifically, in Luke 4:9-11, the devil tempted Jesus to call upon God to deliver him from death in Jerusalem. In this passage, Jesus refused to put God to the test, again quoting scripture to support his position: "Do not put the Lord your God to the test" (Deut 6:16 NRSV) Jesus would eventually face death in Jerusalem, and when he did, he would choose not his own deliverance. Instead, Jesus chose faithfulness to God's will (See Lk 22:42). Jesus response to the devil on the pinnacle of the Temple, therefore, can be seen as a counterpart to his prayer in the Garden of Gethsemane. Jesus would fulfill his divine sonship, not by escaping death, but by accepting death and defeating it (99-100).

According to Baptist scholar Allan Culpepper, the temptation scene serves several important functions in the Gospel of Luke. Two of these functions are foundational for this study. First, the temptations clarified the nature of Jesus' work as the Son of God. In the story of Jesus in the Temple, the baptism of Jesus, and the genealogy of Jesus, Luke developed the case that Jesus of Nazareth was, indeed, "Son of God." The temptations served to interpret the implications of Jesus' identify for his coming ministry. This passage illustrated the fact that Jesus would fulfill the heritage of Israel, combat the rule of Satan, and fulfill his work as Savior by his faithfulness. Second, the temptations offered Jesus' followers a model for resisting temptation. In Luke, Jesus was frequently portrayed as exemplifying characteristically Christian virtues: Jesus was empowered by the Spirit; he prayed regularly; he was compassionate toward the outcast and afflicted; he associated with women, sinners, and tax collectors; and he died a martyr's death, praying for his persecutors. In the temptation scene, Jesus faithfully resisted temptations to be less than or other than he was called to be. He relied on scripture and refused to put God to the test. The temptation story can, therefore, serve as an example story for all disciples of Jesus Christ who are tempted (98).

Connecting with the Story: You Are The Beloved

In the early 1980's, Henri Nouwen and Fred Bratman formed an improbable friendship. At the time, Nouwen, a Catholic priest, noted speaker, and prolific writer, was a member of the faculty of the Yale Divinity School. His extensive writings regarding Christian spirituality, including his noted book, *The Wounded Healer*, had been read and appreciated by millions of people who were seeking a more authentic practice of their Christian faith. Bratman, a young intellectual thoroughly immersed in the secular culture of New York City, was a reporter for the *New York Times*. The two first met when Fred was sent to interview Nouwen for a newspaper article. Although they approached life and matters of faith from entirely different perspectives, over the course of the next several years, the two men became good friends.

Over time, Fred became very familiar with Nouwen's thoughts and writings. As a thoroughly secular person, however, he found it very difficult to relate to the tone and language used in these works. Upon reflection, Nouwen conceded that his writings presupposed a familiarity with certain key concepts and images traditionally associated with the practice of Christian spirituality. Further, he concluded that, in the contemporary context, these concepts and images had lost their power to describe a spirituality that could speak to men and women in a secularized society, persons such as Fred and his friends.

One day, as the two men walked down Columbus Avenue in New York City, Fred turned to Nouwen and said, "Why don't you write something about the spiritual life for me and my friends? You have something to say, but you keep saying it to people who least need to hear it…What about us young, ambitious, secular men and women wondering what life is all about after all? Can you speak to us with the same conviction as you speak to those who share your tradition, your language and your vision?" (Nouwen, 16-17).

Nouwen welcomed this request and eventually wrote a book addressing his concerns. That book, *Life of the Beloved,* is an epistle for the contemporary seeker, an instructional and inspirational letter addressed directly to Fred and his friends. In this book, in simple and direct terms, Nouwen described his understanding of the most intimate truth about all human beings, whether they belong to any particular faith tradition or not. He wrote:

Fred, all I want to say to you is "You are the Beloved," and all I hope is that you can hear these words as spoken to you with all tenderness and force that love can hold. My only desire is to make these words reverberate in every corner of your being—"You are the Beloved."

The greatest gift my friendship can give to you is the gift of your Belovedness. I can give that gift only insofar as I have claimed it for myself. Isn't that what friendship is all about: giving to each other the gift of our Belovedness?

Yes, there is that voice, the voice that speaks from above and from within and that whispers softly or declares loudly: "You are my Beloved, on you my favor rests." (26)

In these tender words of affirmation, Nouwen challenged Fred to accept a new identity as the Beloved of God.

With these words of challenge, Nouwen also offered words of caution. He warned that this unique affirmation of personhood was often masked by other messages from the secular world. He wrote, "It certainly is not easy to hear that voice in a world filled with voices that shout: 'You are no good, you are ugly; you are worthless; you are despicable, you are nobody—unless you demonstrate the opposite'" (26).

Nouwen further maintained that, when people listen to these negative voices, they deny the truth of their Belovedness and fall into what he called "the trap of self-rejection." In acts of self-rejection, some people are tempted to prove their worthiness through the endless pursuit of success, popularity, and power. Others are tempted to become arrogant, inflating their egos in order to hide their real feelings of worthlessness. Still others are tempted to repeat patterns of self-doubt and self-loathing. For Nouwen, the temptation of self-rejection was greatest trap of the secular world, a trap that he encouraged Fred to actively avoid. Further, for Nouwen, self-rejection was also the greatest enemy of the spiritual life because it contradicted the sacred voice that affirms each person as the Beloved. As he exhorted Fred to avoid this trap, he wrote, "Being the Beloved expresses the core truth of our existence" (28).

In his attempt to explain the essence of Christian spirituality to his secular friend, Nouwen implicitly expanded traditional interpretations of the baptism and temptations of Jesus. Nouwen believed that we, as contemporary disciples of Jesus Christ, should share in the meaning and significance of these events.

The same voice that affirmed Jesus at his baptism speaks the same words to all of humanity today: "You are The Beloved, on you my favor rests." The true disciple is about to hear and accept these words of blessing.

Jesus understood these words as an affirmation of his sonship and his unique relationship with God. As followers of Jesus, these words affirm our own Christian identity and our loving relationship with God.

When Jesus was tempted to listen to the voice of the devil, to strive for success, popularity, and power, he stayed true to his own core truth. In similar fashion, when the voices of the secular world tempt us to self-rejection, we must claim and live into our own identity as the Beloved of God.

Resource Page

Read the four Gospel accounts of the baptism of Jesus. As you read, record similarities and differences in these four accounts of the same event.

_____

_____

_____

_____

_____

_____

In Luke 3:22b, a voice from heaven affirmed Jesus' identify: ""You are My Son, the Beloved, with you I am well pleased." Describe the significance of this statement with regard to Jesus' understanding of his own identify.

_____

_____

_____

_____

_____

_____

Biblical scholars have suggested that the baptism of Jesus was really his ordination for ministry. How do you respond to this idea? In what ways do you interpret your own baptism as an ordination for ministry?

_____

_____

_____

_____

_____

_____

Read the four Servant Songs in Isaiah (42:1-4; 49:1-6; 50:4-11; 52:13–53:12). Describe your understanding of how these four texts from Isaiah informed the life and ministry of Jesus of Nazareth.

_____

_____

_____

_____

_____

Read the temptations of Jesus (Lk 4:1-13). Based on your previous studies of this passage, record possible interpretations of the three temptations in the space below.

_____

_____

_____

_____

_____

Based on your reading of the temptation of Jesus, how can a contemporary disciple face the temptation to be less than we are called to be or to do less than we are called to do?

_____

_____

_____

_____

_____

Character Expressed Through a Mission in Life

Focal Passage: Luke 4:14-30

Central Truth of the Lesson

In a time filled with messianic expectations, Jesus began his public ministry with a clear vision of his mission and ministry. This vision grew out of an authentic understanding of his own identify and of his unique relationship with God. At the appropriate time, Jesus publicly declared his identity and the nature of his ministry. Following his example, contemporary disciples of Jesus Christ should approach life with a clearly defined sense of purpose in the world.

Begin with the End in Mind

In his best selling book, *The Seven Habits of Highly Effective People*, leadership consultant Stephen Covey invited his readers to participate in an unusual visualization exercise. He suggested that each reader form a mental picture of his or her own funeral, an event that would take place approximately three years in future. He then encouraged each reader to visualize four persons who would offer eulogies at this funeral: a member of the reader's extended family, a friend, a coworker, and a member of the reader's church or other service organization. With these images clearly established, Covey suggested the following instructions:

Now think deeply. What would you like each of these speakers to say about you and your life? What kind of husband, wife, father, or mother would you like their words to reflect? What kind of son or daughter or cousin? What kind of friend? What kind of working associate?

What character would you like them to have seen in you? What contributions, what achievements would you want them to remember? Look carefully at the people around you. What difference would you like to have made in their lives (Covey, 96-97)?

Covey used this exercise to introduce his second habit of highly effective people: "begin with the end in mind." According to Covey, effective people begin each day with a clear understanding of their ultimate objectives in life. This knowledge serves as a frame of reference by which all daily activities and behaviors are assessed and evaluated. Covey stated, "By keeping the end clearly in mind, you can make certain that whatever you do on any particular day does not violate the criteria you have defined as supremely important, and that each day of your life contributes in a meaningful way to the vision you have of your life as a whole" (98).

In this book, Covey further proposed that the most effective way to "begin with end in mind" was to develop a personal mission statement as a concrete and practical expression of one's ultimate destination in life. A personal mission statement is a carefully worded declaration of:

1) what you want to be, that is, the type of character you wish to embody;
2) what you want to do, or the contributions and achievements that you wish to make; and
3) the core values and principles upon which being and doing are based.

A thoughtfully articulated mission statement functions as a personal compass. In the midst of circumstances and emotions that conspire to seduce a person into a reactive posture, a personal mission statement acts is the foundation for a proactive and intentional approach to life. Daily decisions are made and a mission statement informs short-term goals. Major decisions and long-term goals are also developed, not in light of immediate demands or desires, but with an unmistakable focus on larger aims. Finally, when used as a clear statement of being, doing and valuing, Covey proposed that a personal mission statement could empower an individual with purpose and timeless strength, even in the midst of uncertainty and change (106-8).

Defining a Mission in Anxious Times

As noted in the previous session, Jesus of Nazareth was born in a time characterized by messianic expectations. In the shadow of Roman occupation, many Jewish people eagerly anticipated a messiah who would be a military leader, a man who would expel the Roman legends and establish a new Davidic Kingdom in Jerusalem. Others looked to the prophetic literature for a different understanding of the function of messiah. In The Servant Songs of Isaiah, "The Promised One of Israel" was described as a person who would lead by acts of self-sacrifice, humility, and compassion. Regardless of the understanding of the function, the people of first-century Palestine eagerly awaited the coming of Messiah.

As a first-century Palestinian Jew and as a student of Jewish Scripture, Jesus was most likely aware of the competing expectations associated with the role of messiah. If, however, he did understand himself as the person who would fulfill this role, as the Gospel of Luke clearly indicated, then what type of messiah would he be? In response to this question, Jesus made a series of proactive choices that would ultimately define his mission in life. These choices would often put Jesus at odds with the prevailing expectations of the people in his context.

As described in the first two sessions, Jesus came to a clear understanding of his own identity and of his unique relationship to God. Luke reported that at age twelve, Jesus declared his understanding of this identity and relationship for the first time, to his parents in the Temple. At his baptism, God affirmed this understanding. Then, as demonstrated in his temptations in the desert, Jesus actively resisted enticements to be someone other than God had intended. This sequence of events served a prelude to the beginning of Jesus' public ministry and the announcement of his "mission statement" in the synagogue at Nazareth. This series of events (recorded in Luke 4:14-30) provides the focus of this session.

The Beginning of the Galilean Ministry

In Luke 4:14-15, Luke provided a brief introduction to an extended period of public ministry in the region of Galilee (See Mt 4:12-17 and Mark 1:14-15 for parallel accounts). As described in the remainder of the fourth chapter, the activities associated with this ministry were concentrated in two towns in the region: Capernaum and Nazareth, Jesus' hometown. Scholars have suggested that this two-verse prologue functions as a point of transition, in both activity and location, in the flow of the Gospel narrative (Craddock, 60).

This passage also foreshadows two important aspects of Luke's understanding of Jesus' mission and ministry. First, as described in the Third Gospel, Jesus was, at heart, a rabbi—a well respected and admired teacher. To that end, a major portion of his mission in life would be defined in terms of a ministry of teaching (Culpepper, 103). Second, as recorded in the Gospel of Luke, this ministry of teaching would be centered, at least in the early stages of his ministry, in local synagogues. Eventually, Jesus' ongoing conflict with the religious leaders who governed these synagogues would force him to find other contexts in which to teach. But at this stage of his ministry, Jesus was a very popular guest teacher in these local centers of learning and worship (Tolbert, 44).

In this passage, Luke also wanted his readers to know the people's initial reaction to Jesus and to his teaching: "he was praised by everyone" (Lk 4:15b, NRSV). This passage was not an isolated example of this type of affirmation. In fact, the universal acclaim of Jesus was a major theme in the Gospel of Luke. The book is filled with stories in which the people responded to his authoritative teaching with awe and amazement (Culpepper, 103) (See Lk 4:22, 6:19, and 9:43 for only a few examples). In a short period of time, Jesus was becoming the center of attention in the region (Tolbert, 44). It is, however, important to note that this universal acclaim and popularity would quickly be called into question in, of all places, Jesus' hometown and home synagogue. The affirmation of the people in Luke 4:15b stands in sharp contrast to the violent rejection by his own townspeople in Luke 4:28-29 (Craddock, 60).

Homecoming

In Luke 4:16-30, a passage often identified as the rejection of Jesus at Nazareth, this popular rabbi and regional "celebrity-in-the-making" traveled back to his hometown for a visit. Parallel passages describing this event, or a similar event, are found in Mark 6:1-6 and in Matthew 4:13. In these parallel accounts, the Gospel writers reported that Jesus had been involved in an extended period of ministry in Galilee before returning home to Nazareth. In Luke's account of the homecoming experience, however, the writer reported that this visit occurred at the beginning of Jesus' work in the region. When the Synoptic Gospels differ in the chronology of specific events, biblical scholars speculate that an individual writer might have rearranged the order of these actual events in order to support a thematic emphasis in that particular Gospel. In this instance, scholars believe that Luke included this homecoming visit at this point in his narrative to further develop a particular theme addressed in the preceding stories. In the story of Jesus in the Temple (Lk 2:41-52), the baptism of Jesus (Lk 3:21-22), the genealogy of Jesus (Lk 3:23-38), and the temptations of Jesus (Lk 4:1-13), Luke established the fact that Jesus had a *personal* understanding of his own identity and of his unique relationship with God. In the flow of Luke's narrative, it was now time to for this understanding to be made *public*. The homecoming story, and its unique position in the narrative, announced who Jesus was, described the nature of his ministry, and foreshadowed the public response to both Jesus and his ministry (61).

Synagogue, Sabbath, and Scripture

In Luke 4:16, the Gospel writer reported that, on the Sabbath, Jesus went to synagogue, "as was his practice." In his portrayal of Jesus as a man who regularly participated in established traditions and practices, Luke wanted to establish the fact that Jesus, like the members of his immediate family, was a faithful and pious Jew, a person well-grounded in the Three S's of the Jewish Faith: Synagogue, Sabbath, and Scripture (61).

First created during the period of the Babylonian Exile, the synagogue was, at the time of Jesus, the institutional center of the Jewish faith. While significant festivals and holy days were celebrated at the Temple in Jerusalem, the local synagogue was the primary context in which ordinary Jewish people, folks like Jesus and his family, regularly practiced the traditions of the faith. In the synagogue in Nazareth, Jesus' family and neighbors, gathered weekly for Sabbath worship. In this synagogue, Jesus, as a typical Jewish boy, learned how to read and to interpret Scripture. This synagogue most likely functioned as a community center—a site for large meals, weddings, and other fellowship activities. While the priests conducted worship in the Temple, the synagogue was a lay-led institution. Men in the town took turns facilitating the various functions associated with this synagogue. According to commentator Fred Craddock, Jesus must have had a special place in his heart for this place and for the people who gathered there: "Among relatives and friends, in the synagogue Jesus is at home" (62).

The liturgy, or order of worship, associated with weekly Sabbath worship probably included the following elements. First, the *Shema* (Deut 6:4-6), the Decalogue (the Ten Commandments), and eighteen specific prayers of benediction were recited. A member of the congregation would then be asked to stand and to read a specific portion of the Torah (in Hebrew). Next, a worshiper would be asked to stand and to read a selection from the Psalms or the Prophets (also in Hebrew). The person asked to perform this reading was often allowed to choose the specific text that he would read (Gilmour, 89). One of the readers would then sit down in front of the congregation and offer exposition of and commentary on the Scriptures (in the vernacular language of the region, in this case, Aramaic). The service would end with a final blessing and the collection of alms for the poor (Culpepper, 105).

In Luke 4:16b-17, Luke reported that Jesus was invited to participate in worship by reading a portion of Scripture. The *hazzan*, or worship assistant, gave Jesus a copy of a scroll containing the words of the Prophet Isaiah. Exercising his prerogative to select a passage of his own choosing, Jesus unrolled the scroll and found a particular text to read.

Jesus' First Sermon: A Personal Mission Statement

The verses that Jesus read, here recorded in Luke 4:18-19, served as the scripture text for what has come to be known as Jesus' inaugural sermon. These two verses were a modified version of Isaiah 61:1-2 (one of the Servant Songs) and Isaiah 58:6.

> The Spirit of the Lord is upon me,
> because he has anointed me
> to bring good news to the poor.
> He has sent me to proclaim release to the captives
> and recovery of sight to the blind,
> to let the oppressed go free.
> to proclaim the year of the Lord's favor.

Following the reading, Jesus rolled up the scroll, gave it back to the attendant, and sat down in front of the other worshippers. By tradition, Jesus was expected to share his interpretation of the passage that he had selected and read. In light of his familial connections and of his growing reputation as a great rabbi, the members of his hometown synagogue were, most likely, eager to hear what he might say. In fact, in verse 20, Luke reported the fact that "The eyes of all in the synagogue were fixed on him." Then, in verse 21, Luke recorded the first words of Jesus' public ministry: "Today this scripture has been fulfilled in your hearing."

What was the significance of these passages from Isaiah, read in this special place, at this particular point in Jesus' ministry? According to Commentator Fred Craddock, the purpose was twofold. First, Jesus wanted to *publicly* declare what he had already *privately* accepted. Here, in front of family and friends, Jesus used Scripture to announce his understanding of his own identity and of his special relationship with God. With the experiences of his baptism and his temptations in the wilderness serving as a backdrop, Jesus quoted Scripture to declare that, today, he had been anointed, literally "made messiah," by the Spirit of the Lord. Second, having made this declaration, Jesus went on to describe the nature of his anointing and the focus of his ministry. In his selection of this passage, Jesus ignored the popular expectation that messiah might be a military leader. Instead, he chose to identify with Isaiah's suffering servant, a messiah who was concerned with self-sacrifice, humility, and compassion. Furthermore, he declared his intention to associate with and minister to all types of people living on the margins of acceptable society—the poor, the captives, the blind, and the oppressed (Craddock, 62).

An additional insight from the selected passages was noted. In Luke 4:19, Jesus declared that a part of his ministry would be "to proclaim the year of the Lord's favor." Biblical scholars believed that this phrase referred to the Jewish celebration of the Year of Jubilee (as described in Lev 25:8-17). In this passage, the people of Israel were instructed that, every fiftieth year, they should "proclaim liberty throughout the land," return all property to the family that originally owed that land, and avoid all cultivation of the land, eating "only what the field itself produces." Although the Jewish people rarely followed these instructions to the "letter of the Law," the concept of Jubilee came to represent a time of amnesty, liberation, and restoration in the Jewish faith. By speaking these words in this context, some commentators believe that Jesus further expanded this concept. In essence, he declared that the principles of Jubilee have been fulfilled, today, as he declared not only his own mission, but also the character of the Kingdom of God (Culpepper, 106).

How did the people in the synagogue respond to Jesus' personal mission statement, to this bold declaration of identity and mission? Shock and awe might be appropriate terms to describe the emotional dynamics at work in the synagogue of Nazareth on that day.

In verse 22, the tension was evident. On one hand, the crowd was amazed at the eloquence of the messenger and the message. On the other hand, Jesus' commentary was greeted with varying degrees of skepticism depending on how the question, "Is not this Joseph's son?" is interpreted by the reader. Regardless of the reader's understanding of the mood of the room, one fact was clear: Jesus' interpretation of these verse differed sharply from what those gathered in the synagogue assumed that they meant (106). Sensing the range of reactions at work in the synagogue, Jesus moved to further clarify his interpretation of the passages.

In the text of his sermon (Lk 4:23-27), Jesus addressed the high expectations associated with his rising reputation and his return to his hometown. Commentators generally agree that people of Nazareth had heard about Jesus' ministry in Capernaum, a neighboring area in Galilee that happened to have a large Gentile population. These commentators also speculate that Jesus' family and friends eagerly anticipated his homecoming and the great signs that he would do in their presence. The people of Nazareth reasoned, "If Jesus can accomplish great things in that place, with *those* people, just image the mighty works he will perform when he comes back home!" When Jesus failed to produce these mighty acts, the people of his hometown were, at the very least, disappointed. In the synagogue on that Sabbath day, some of the people probably experienced a sense of jealousy or resentment (Craddock, 63). While the exact meaning of the phrase, "Doctor, cure yourself!" (See Lk 4:23) is a matter of much conjecture, the notion that "no prophet is accepted in the prophet's hometown" (see Lk 4:24 and parallel references in Mk 6:4, Mt 13:57, and Jn 4:44) does directly address this implied jealousy and resentment.

In Luke 4:25-27, Jesus continued to defend his ministry among the non-Jewish people in Capernaum and his inactivity in Nazareth by telling his audience of two stories from Jewish Scripture. As recorded in I Kings 17:8-14, Jesus reminded his audience that, in the midst of a famine, Elijah provided food for a Gentile widow. Also, in II Kings 5:1-17, Elisha was instrumental in healing Naaman, a Gentile leper who was the commander of an opposing army. In sharing these stories, Jesus was quick to point to the fact that these two great prophets offered aid to these Gentiles, even though many Jewish persons were also in need of assistance. When the worshipers in the synagogue were faced with this frank re-interpretation of their own Scripture, resentment and jealousy turned into anger and violence. Their actions were reported in Luke 4:28-30. Filled with rage, they drove their hometown "hero-in-the-making" out of town, toward the brow of a hill. Their intent was to end his life. Miraculously, Jesus passed through the midst of the angry crowd. Probably with disappointment in his heart, Jesus left his hometown, determined to live into his identify and to live out the ministry goals that he had just declared.

The Mission Statement of the Disciple of Jesus Christ

In times of uncertainty and change, when demands and expectations are high, people need a personal compass—a trustworthy instrument that can be used to prioritize the demands of daily life, to make informed decisions, to respond to crises, to set long-term goals, and to plan for a productive future. As a self-aware individual, as a member of a growing family, and as a business consultant, Stephen Covey understands this need and has had much success in helping others to address this need. In his best selling books and in his training seminars, Covey encourages people to "begin with the end in mind," that is, to develop a clear vision of one's ultimate character, achievements, and values. He also coaches his readers and conference participants to develop personal, family, and organizational mission statements. These mission statements would serve as practical tools to help them realize their vision for the future.

Long before Covey's work was published, the writer of the Gospel of Luke also understood the dynamics at work in these processes of defining self and articulating a mission. Based on his desire to provide "an orderly account of the events" in Jesus' life, Luke crafted a series of stories demonstrating how Jesus first discovered and claimed an unshakeable understanding of his own identity and of his unique relationship with God. Next, this understanding was affirmed at his baptism and tested during the temptations in the wilderness. At the right time, Jesus felt compelled to publicly announce his identity and describe the nature of his mission in life. In the context of his hometown synagogue, Jesus used Scripture to publicly articulate his personal mission statement (and perhaps the mission statement of his church) in his inaugural sermon. Finally, Jesus' self-definition and declaration of an inclusive ministry led to both praise and rejection by members of his community. In spite of these mixed reactions, Jesus remained true to himself and to his mission in life.

Following his example, the contemporary disciple of Jesus Christ should:

- develop an unshakeable understanding of the person that he or she has been created by God to be, in Jesus Christ;
- seek a growing relationship with God through Jesus Christ;
- listen to God's affirmations of this identity and this relationship;
- articulate his or her mission in life, i.e., identify the contributions that he or she can make to the Kingdom of God and the achievements that he or she can accomplish in the name of God;
- announce this identity and mission, in both word and deed; and expect mixed reactions from family, friends, and colleagues.

To follow Jesus Christ on the path of self-definition and intentional ministry is, indeed, the essence of Christian character and discipleship. Based on a clear sense of being, doing and valuing, the disciple of Jesus Christ is empowered with purpose and timeless strength, even in the midst of uncertainty and change.

Resource Page

Record your impressions regarding the thoughts and feelings that Jesus might have experienced as he anticipated his homecoming and the public announcement of his identity and mission.

_____
_____
_____
_____
_____
_____

Record your impressions regarding the thoughts and feelings that the people of Nazareth might have experienced as they anticipated Jesus' homecoming.

_____
_____
_____
_____
_____
_____

Read Luke 4:18-19, Luke's version of the text Jesus read during worship in the synagogue at Nazareth. Next, read Isaiah 58:6 and Isaiah 62:1-2, the two passages quoted in verse 18 and 19. In the space below, compare and contrast the two readings. In your opinion, what is the significance of the differences in these two readings?

_____

_____

_____

_____

_____

Based on your reading of Luke 4:18-19, describe your understanding of the nature of Jesus' ministry.

_____

_____

_____

_____

_____

Read Luke 4:20-26. How would you characterize the initial reaction of the worshipers to Jesus' statement of identity and mission? Describe your understanding of why the worshipers in the synagogue at Nazareth became so angry with Jesus.

_____

_____

_____

_____

To what extent does your understanding of your personal mission reflect your commitment to Jesus Christ? To what extent does your understanding of your personal mission reflect your commitment to ministry with others in the name of Jesus Christ?

_____

_____

_____

_____

Character Developed Through Time Well-Invested

Central Truth of the Session

The life and ministry of Jesus as described in the Gospel of Luke demonstrate the fact that Jesus invested his time wisely. Based on a clear understanding of his unique relationship with God and of his mission in life, Jesus devoted time to enriching his own spiritual life, to establishing relationships with people, and to participating in acts of ministry and service to others. To that end, Jesus lived a life that was centered, balanced, and meaningful.

Background for this Session

The insights included in this session were developed through an inductive study of the Gospel of Luke. What is an inductive Bible study? In an inductive study of the Bible, the facilitator and the class participants select a specific topic or a large section of scripture as the focus of their study. If a specific topic is selected, the leader and the learners use a concordance to identify all references to that topic in the scriptures. When these passages have been identified, participants read every selection. If a large section of scripture (such as The Gospel of Luke) is chosen for the study, then the participants read the entire selection. In either case, the learners look for specific details in the texts: characters, images, words, ideas, and symbols. These details are noted in a reading journal. Next, the participants review the information in the journal, combining specific details to form general impressions and ideas about the passages. Common themes and principles emerge as the learners continue to work with these specific details. Through a process of discovery learning, participants in inductive Bible studies develop a deeper understanding of and appreciation for the topic or scriptural passages chosen for the study.

In preparation for this study, which was originally taught as a Lenten Bible study at Fredericksburg Baptist Church in Fredericksburg, Virginia, I read the entire Gospel of Luke several times. With each reading, I explored a different theme related to the character of the disciple as embodied in and modeled by Jesus Christ. One of these general themes was the manner in which Jesus invested his time in his own spiritual development, in the lives of others, and in his ministry of teaching and healing. This session is designed not only to discovery how Jesus invested his time. It will also provide an overview of the entire Gospel of Luke and an introduction to the next six sessions in the study. Several of the biblical passages introduced in this session will be studied in more detail in subsequent sessions in this study.

As you prepare for your class discussion of this session, I encourage you to conduct your own inductive study of the Gospel of Luke. You should be able to read the entire book in one to two hours. As you read, keep a journal, recording details about how Jesus spent his time in these narratives. Then, compare the results of your study to the material included in this session. If you do not choose to read the entire book, read the passages used to illustrate each of the concepts included in the lesson. In either case, focus on the question: Based on your reading of the Gospel of Luke, what principles and patterns regarding the use of time do you see at work in the life and ministry of Jesus?

Time Invested in Waiting

As described in the first session of this series, biblical scholars have speculated that Jesus already had at least of a basic understanding of his unique relationship with God by age twelve. For whatever reason, Jesus chose to delay the time when he would begin to live into the implications of this relationship, at least in a public context. In Luke 3:23, the writer of the Gospel indicated that Jesus began his public ministry at age thirty, some eighteen years later. How did Jesus spend his time in these missing years? This question has been the source of much debate in scholarly circles. Did he continue to explore his own identity? Did he develop a deeper understanding of his relationship with God? Did he spend time studying the scripture in the local synagogue or in the Temple in Jerusalem? Did he work with his father as a carpenter in Nazareth? Did he take on family responsibilities associated with being a first-born Jewish male? Did he have a close relationship with John the Baptist, his relative and forerunner? Did Jesus go to the desert to live with the ascetic Essenes in the Qumran community? We can only speculate on where Jesus was and what he did during these years. One thing is certain: Jesus chose to wait. He waited for the appropriate time to fulfill his mission in a public context.

Time Invested in Retreat

In the Gospel of Luke, various narratives demonstrated that Jesus was a very busy person, constantly on the move from village to village, constantly surrounded by disciples and crowds of curious people. The narratives also indicated that, at critical junctures in his active life, Jesus chose to withdraw from the busyness. Periods of activity were balanced by periods of retreat.

Sometimes, Jesus retreated in order to be alone. As discussed in the second session of this series, immediately after his baptism, Jesus withdrew to a desert place for forty days. During this time of discipline and discernment, he was tempted to reinterpret his mission in life (See Lk 4:1-13). In Luke 4:42, Luke indicated that, after a busy season of ministry, Jesus moved to an isolated place for time alone. A third example of a personal retreat was reported in Luke 6:12. In this passage, Jesus climbed a mountain and prayed all night prior to the naming of the twelve. This important pattern of personal retreat before significant events and important decisions continued throughout his public ministry.

At other times, Jesus retreated from his public ministry to spend time in the company of his disciples. These small group experiences were often very meaningful moments in the lives of Jesus and his disciples. Further, significant teachings often emerged from these experiences. In Luke 9:18-27, Jesus was alone with the disciples, having conversation and asking questions. In this context, Peter confessed that Jesus was "The Messiah of God." In Luke 9:28-36, the transfiguration, Jesus, Peter, James, and John shared a unique and powerful epiphany. In Luke 11:1-13, the writer of the Gospel described a small group experience in which one of Jesus' disciples asked to teach them how to pray. Jesus' response to this request was the model prayer. And finally, in Luke 22:39-47, Jesus prayed in the Garden of Gethsemane with his sleeping disciples close at hand.

Time Invested in Friends and Supporters

In the Gospel of Luke, the term "disciples" was often used to designate a broader circle of Jesus' associates and friends. These people became his support network as he participated in ministry.

The story recorded in Luke 8:1-3 illustrated the diverse community of individuals that accompanied Jesus in his travels. In addition to his specially selected group of twelve male associates, a number of women were a part of Jesus' entourage. Jesus had healed many of these women and, in gratitude, they provided support for his work. The women listed in the scriptures represented very different segments of first century society. From Mary Magdalene, once demon-possessed and living on the edges of acceptable society, to Joanna, the wife of a Roman official, these women were intimate associates of Jesus and eyewitnesses to his life and ministry.

As a single adult living at some great distance from his family, Jesus enjoyed the companionship of families who graciously opened their homes to him. Jesus shared a similar experience in the home of Mary, Martha, and Lazarus. In Luke 10:38-42, Mary, Martha, and Lazarus offered friendship and hospitality to Jesus and his disciples.

Time Invested in His Mission in Life:
Teaching and Healing

A basic premise of this study is the assumption that Jesus understood his mission in life in terms of a ministry of teaching and healing. If this hypothesis is correct, it would only make sense that he would invest a great deal of time and energy in activities associated with this type of ministry. A careful reading of the Gospel of Luke supported this assumption.

In first-century Jewish culture, the task of teaching boys and men to read and interpret the scriptures was centered in the local synagogue. It would have been quite natural for Jesus, a respected Jewish rabbi, to regularly teach in these houses of learning. In Luke 4:31-44, we find two instances of Jesus teaching in local synagogues.

Jesus also invested a great deal of time in teaching his disciples about the demands of discipleship. Immediately after naming the twelve, Jesus gathered his larger circle of disciples and a multitude of other people for lessons in the nature of discipleship. His teaching was recorded in Luke 6:17-49, the Sermon on the Plain, a parallel passage to the Sermon on the Mount recorded in Matthew 5-7.

Beginning in Luke 8, Jesus initiated an extended period of itinerant ministry, teaching and healing "on the fly." Rather than establishing himself in a central location and encouraging the sick or potential followers to come to him, Jesus made himself accessible the people as he traveled from village to village. As his reputation grew, crowds followed him on his journeys. The parable of the Sower, found in Luke 8:4-8, was shared with his disciples and a large crowd at the beginning of this "ministry by walking around."

Jesus attempted to instruct his critics. Early in his ministry, representatives of the religious establishment were very curious about Jesus and his ministry. They joined the crowds of other curious people who flocked to hear his teachings and to witness his acts of healings. One such incident was recorded in Luke 5:17-26. When Jesus began to publicly proclaim his unique relationship with God and to heal under the authority of that relationship, his relationship with these religious leaders quickly became adversarial. In fact, in the latter stages of his ministry, these leaders intentionally asked questions and presented situations designed to entrap Jesus. In spite of these hostile purposes, Jesus continued to offer words of instruction, even to his worst critics. For example, in Luke 15:1-32, Jesus shared a series of three parables—the Lost Coin, the Lost Sheep, and the Lost Son—to challenge conventional religious wisdom of the religious leaders.

The Gospel of Luke is also a powerful testimony to the fact that Jesus fulfilled his mission in life through a ministry of healing. Through this work, Jesus associated with and restored many persons living on the margins of acceptable society. In Luke 7:1-10, Jesus healed the slave of a Roman centurion. In Luke 7:11-17, near the town of Nain, Jesus resuscitated the son of a widow. In Luke 8:26-39, Jesus exorcised a man living among the tombs in the country of the Gerasenes. In Luke 8:40-48, Jesus healed a woman who was perpetually unclean due to hemorrhages. In Luke 13:10-17, Jesus healed a cripple woman on the Sabbath, facing the ire of the synagogue leaders as a result of this act of kindness. And in Luke 17:11-19, Jesus encountered ten lepers, persons required by Jewish law to live apart from society. He healed them and empowered them to move from the margins of society back to life in community with others.

In many of these examples, Jesus integrated acts of healing with his teaching ministry.

Time Invested "At Table"

As described in the introduction to this study, many narratives chronicled in the Gospel of Luke are set in the context of meals. In these stories, Jesus shared meals with a variety of people.

In Luke 5:27-32, Jesus was invited to the house of Levi, his disciple and a former tax collector. He shared a meal with Levi and his friends, persons described as "tax collectors and sinners." In Luke 19:1-10, Jesus even invited himself to the home for another tax collector, Zacchaeus. By sharing food and intimate fellowship with these questionable characters, Jesus broke the social and religious conventions of the day. His presence at these dinners was a demonstration that Jesus was willing to set aside convention in order to establish intimate relationship with persons "in need of a physician."

In Luke 9:10-17, Jesus created community and addressed the physical needs of the crowds in the Feeding of the 5000, an event so important in the ministry of Jesus that it was recorded in all four Gospels.

On several occasions, various religious leaders invited Jesus to their houses for a meal. Many of these meals precipitated confrontations between Jesus and his hosts. In Luke 7:36-50, much to the chagrin of his host, Jesus welcomed and forgave a notorious woman who anointed him. In Luke 11:37-54, his host criticized Jesus' table manners and received a sharp rebuke from his guest. Again, in Luke 14:1-24, in the context of a festive celebration at the home of important leaders of the Pharisees, Jesus offered criticized the behavior of the party guests and offered pointed instruction about the nature of true devotion and discipleship.

Jesus also celebrated intimate meals associated with religious festivals with his disciples. Luke 22:7-38 described the celebration of Passover and institution of the Eucharist.

Time Spent in Conflict

According to conventional wisdom, Jesus should have reserved his harshest words of criticism and judgment for sinners and persons of dubious character. This was not the case in the Gospel of Luke; in fact, the opposite was true. Fully aware of both their sinfulness and their pain, Jesus offered relationship and unconditional acceptance to sinners and marginalized persons. Further, according to conventional wisdom, Jesus should have praised the piety and religious discipline of the established religious leaders of his day. Again, the opposite was true. Jesus uttered stinging words of rebuke to the scribes, the Pharisees, and the Sadducees. In addition to the meal-time conflicts previously described, Jesus was often in open and hostile conflict with these leaders, particularly in the latter stages of his ministry.

In Luke 19:45-47, in an affront to the authority of the religious establishment, Jesus drove the merchants out of the Temple complex.

In Luke 20, the writer of the Gospel described a series of confrontations between Jesus and the religious leaders, each confrontation more intense than the one preceding it. In these heated arguments, the religious leaders openly questioned Jesus' authority and actively tried to entrap him in some accusable offense.

Principles and Patterns for Investing Time

In the research associated with this session, I identified a number of significant principles and patterns associated with the manner in which Jesus chose to invest his time. These principles and patterns, when applied to our own understanding of Christian discipleship, challenge us as contemporary followers of Jesus Christ to reconsider the ways in which we choose to invest the precious commodity of time.

First, the scriptures indicated that Jesus lived a centered life. All of his values, beliefs, attitudes, and actions revolved around a core defined in term of Jesus' understanding of his own identity and on his unique relationship to God. In the Gospel of Luke, being preceded doing, for both Jesus and his followers. In his book, *A Serious Call to a Contemplative Lifestyle*, Glenn Hinson explains the concept of the "centered life" in very practical terms. Hinson suggests that, if contemporary disciples of Jesus Christ ever hope to regain control of our hectic lives, we must discover an integrative center from which to establish a different kind of rapport with God, with the world, and the society of people around us. Hinson defines this center in his paraphrase of Matthew 6:33: "Seek first the kingdom of God and God's okaying of you, and all these things (food, clothing, shelter) shall fall into place for you"(Hinson, 58-59). If our lives find focus in God's affirmation of our personhood and in our desire to participate in the Kingdom of God, a whole new constellation of priorities and values may emerge. Ultimately, our investment of time may also be radically altered.

Second, Jesus invested his time based on a clear understanding of his mission in life, a mission defined in terms of teaching and healing. From the beginning of his public ministry, when Jesus began to articulate his understanding of his mission, through his post-resurrection appearances to his disciples, the majority of the stories recorded in the Gospel of Luke illustrated this unique mission. What can contemporary disciples can learn from Jesus' mission-centered approach to life?

Based on a growing understanding of our personal identity and our relationship with God, we should articulate our own mission statement, clearly defining our purpose in life.

We must explore ways to accomplish this mission as we face the demands of daily life. Today, our lives are often defined in terms of a continuous series of seemingly unrelated events that demand our time. Jobs, household chores, child-rearing tasks, and a plethora of other worthy activities must be accomplished during the course of the day. How can these everyday activities relate to God's will for our lives and contribute to God's ultimate purposes?

At a time when our lives are often compartmentalized, a mission statement can bring both purpose and integrity to life.

Finally, Jesus led a balanced life. His use of time in the Gospel of Luke embodied the scriptural truth that, "to everything there is a time and a purpose under heaven." In these stories, Jesus balanced

- periods of engagement in ministry and periods of retreat and spiritual formation;
- time with large groups of people in ministry and time alone in prayer;
- time with his friends and supporters and time with his inner circle;
- time in celebration with people at dinner and time confronting his critics at meals; and
- time with the prominent religious leaders and time with people on the margins of society.

In a context in which contemporary disciples of Jesus are tempted to spend the bulk of time on work, with little focus on family, recreation, spiritual renewal, and service to others, Jesus' example of a balanced use of time is indeed a challenge.

Fourth, Jesus did not just spend time; he invested time. The stories recorded in the Gospel of Luke illustrated that Jesus invested time in his own spiritual formation and relationship with God. He also invested a great deal of time in people—healing them, challenging them, and equipping them for service and ministry on behalf of the Kingdom of God. As a contemporary discipleship of Jesus Christ, do you spend time or do you invest time? Again, Glenn Hinson offers words of practical advice regarding the wise use of time. He states that the major issue today is not a problem of having time; rather it is an issue of using time meaningfully. As we assess our use of time, Hinson suggests that we ask two questions:

"Why am I doing this?" and
"Is this activity meaningful?" (63-64)

The first question addresses purpose and mission; the second question deals with impact. Jesus Christ embodied and called us to embody the meaningful investment of time.

Resource Page

One of our most important documents is our calendar. Take a moment to review the activities in which you participated during the past month as record in your PDA or organizer. List the top ways in which you spent the majority of your time during the past month.

_____

_____

_____

_____

_____

_____

After reviewing your calendar, use the following scale to assess your investment of time in the following areas:
    3—I invested a great amount of time in this type of activity.
    2—I invested some time in this type of activity.
    1—I invested very little time in this type of activity.

Time Invested in Prayer_____
Time Invested in Rest_____
Time Invested in Meaningful Recreation_____
Time Invested with Family Members_____
Time Invested with Spiritual Friends_____
Time Invested in Meaningful Work_____
Time Invested in Fulfilling Your Mission in Life_____
Time Invested in Food and Fellowship_____

Based on your assessments, name one specific strategy or activity which might improve your investment of time.

_____

_____

_____

_____

_____

_____

Recall a significant period of spiritual retreat. Describe that experience and its significance in your own spiritual formation.

_____

_____

_____

_____

_____

_____

Who is your most significant spiritual friend? Why is this relationship important to you? How much time have you spent with this person during the last month?

_____

_____

_____

_____

_____

_____

Character Developed Through Intimate Relationships

Central Truth of the Session

As recorded in the Gospel of Luke, Jesus chose to live with the people who responded to his invitation to follow him. In the context of day-to-day living, Jesus embodied the Gospel message and modeled complete dependence on God for his close friends and associates.

Ministry through the Back Door

In August 1981, I moved to Louisville, Kentucky, to begin what eventually became a long tenure as a student at The Southern Baptist Theological Seminary. In July 1982, I was called to serve as Minister of Youth at First Baptist Church, Bedford, Indiana. This post was a "part-time" position that would allow me to continue my studies while gaining valuable ministry experience. For the next two and one-half years, I got into my car each Friday afternoon for the seventy-mile commute to Bedford, ministered with the youth and their families over the weekend, and then returned to Louisville on Monday afternoon to begin another week of formal theological studies.

During my first few months at First Baptist, my weekend home was a small, rented room in downtown Bedford. As a confirmed introvert, I treasured the privacy provided by this arrangement. As a poor seminary student, however, I soon realized that I could not afford the luxury of a personal space. When I shared my dilemma with the leaders of the church, the chair of the deaconesses generously suggested an option. She agreed to ask different families in the congregation to provide food and lodging for me on the weekend. The plan was that each family would host me for one month of weekends; then I would move on to the next family. Reluctantly, I agreed to this arrangement. It was one of the best decisions of my life.

During my time in Bedford, I lived with a wide variety of families—senior adult widows, retired couples, the family of one of the other ministers in the church, and, most memorably, the families of the church with youth involved in my ministry. In these of each of these households, I learned an important lesson: it is one thing to minister with people from a distance; it is quite another thing to live with the folks with whom you minister.

After a few months in the rotation, I developed two basic approaches to my weekend stays. With some of these families, I felt the need to maintain my ministerial persona at all times. In these situations, my hosts treated me as "the guest minister," displaying their best manners, forcing their children to be on their best behavior, cooking special meals served in formal contexts, and feeling an obligation to entertain me. While in these households, I dutifully played the expected role and actively looked for opportunities to go to my office at the church for a few moments of respite. In some of these homes, I ultimately spent more time and energy playing the role of minister than I did in developing relationships with my hosts.

My fondest memories of these days were weekends spent in households in which I was viewed both as a minister of the church *and* an adopted member of the family. In these families, I was viewed as a spiritual leader of the church, but I was also encouraged to walk in the back door, without ringing the bell. I was invited to breakfast in my pajamas and robe, before I showered. I ate at the kitchen table, not the dining room table. I did not have to make polite conversation. At times, I could just sit quietly and the family would know that "Tim needs some space." At other times, I would often stay up late into the night with the youth and their parents, arguing politics and discussing how we should live out our faith. When a parent and a youth argued in front of me and did not expect me to take sides in the argument, I knew that I was truly a part of the family. In these households, I experienced a level of intimacy that few ministers ever achieve. In these intimate relationships, I was able to *be* a minister, not to play the role of a minister.

When I began doctoral studies at Southern, I was called to serve a church in Louisville. Since graduation, I have ministered in two other congregations, each larger and more prestigious than the Bedford congregation. But the people with whom I lived and ministered in Indiana continued to invite me to participate in their lives. I visit Bedford regularly, staying in the same homes. I have participated in the weddings of six of the youth with whom I ministered. I have celebrated the births of their children, my "grandchildren." When I had surgery in 2000, I asked to be on their church prayer list. I attended the funeral of one of my "Bedford moms." And in times of transition and crisis, members of my extended family at Bedford still contact me for words of encouragement and advice. To this day, I consider my time with the folks at First Baptist Bedford to be my most effective years of ministry.

Exploring Biblical Truth: Invited to Follow

Many of the stories recorded in the Gospel of Luke demonstrated the truth that "it is one thing to minister with people from a distance; it is quite another thing to live with the folks with whom you minister."

In the early days of Jesus' public ministry, a multitude of people gathered wherever he went. Some of these folks came to hear his teaching because he taught with unique authority. Others came to experience healing or to witness a miracle. As he traveled from place to place, some individuals in the crowd began to follow Jesus, literally. Others began a part of a network of supporters and friends. In Gospel of Luke, all of these people were called "disciples." Before and after the naming of the twelve apostles, Jesus took initiative to establish relationships with and to call out disciples.

In Luke 4:38-41, after teaching in the synagogue, Simon Peter opened this home to Jesus. When they discovered that Simon's mother-in-law was ill, Jesus healed her. In appreciation, she got up from her sickbed and helped prepare a meal! After dinner, Simon's house became a ministry center as the sick of the community came to Jesus for healing.

In Luke 5:1-11, Jesus invited Peter, James, and John to leave behind their profession of fishing to accept the vocation of "fishing for men." In spite of Simon's self-professed sinfulness, the three immediately joined Jesus.

In Luke 5:27-39, Jesus invited Levi, a hated tax collector, to follow him. In gratitude for this act of acceptance, Levi threw a party and invited Jesus to meet his friends and associates.

In Luke 8:2-3, Jesus and the twelve were joined by a company of women. Some of these women, including Mary Magdalene, had experienced healing through the ministry of Jesus. In gratitude, they traveled with Jesus and his inner circle, "providing for them out of their resources."

In Luke 10:38-42, Jesus is a guest at the home of Mary and Martha. Although the exact nature of their relationship was not described in the Gospel of Luke, John 11:1-44 details a close and intimate rapport among Jesus, Mary, Martha, and their brother Lazarus. In the passage from John, Jesus responded to the illness and death of Lazarus with compassion and miraculous restoration.

Invited to Intimate Relationship

In the focal passages selected for this lesson, Jesus sought a more intimate level of relationship with some of his followers. From the larger body of "disciples," Jesus chose to select a smaller group of people with whom he would relate more closely. The calling of the twelve is found in Luke 6:12-16. The scripture reported that the selection of the twelve was preceded by such an extended period of prayer. Jesus spent the entire night in an isolated, mountainous place, asking for God's guidance. The following morning, Jesus gathered the larger body of his disciples and announced that he had selected twelve people to be "apostles." In addition to Simon, James, John, and Levi, Jesus picked Andrew, Simon's brother, Philip, Bartholomew, Thomas, James the son of Alphaeus, Simon the Zealot, Judas the son of James, and Judas Iscariot.

Immediately after they were selected, Jesus and the twelve came down from the mountain and joined the rest of the disciples and a large multitude of people on a nearby plain. In the hearing of all these people, Jesus began the training of the twelve. His words of instruction are found in Luke 6:17-45, a passage known as the Teachings on the Plain. In this passage, and in its parallel passage in the Gospel of Matthew, the Sermon on the Mount, Jesus used inspiring words and powerful images to describe the nature of discipleship and the character of the disciple.

In the days that followed, the twelve traveled with Jesus, watching and learning as Jesus modeled the principles of discipleship, ministered to the needs of people, and faced criticism from religious leaders. When the time was right, Jesus entrusted the twelve with his ministry. In Luke 9:1-6, he empowered and commissioned the twelve to proclaim the Kingdom of God and to heal the people. In these verses, Jesus also described a character trait that would be necessary to accomplish this mission—*complete dependence on God*. As Jesus sent the twelve, they were instructed to take no provisions, no money, or no extra clothes. Just as Jesus trusted God to provide for his needs, the twelve were challenged to rely completely on God for their livelihood. In Luke 10:1-12, Jesus commissioned a larger group of seventy disciples to the same mission, with the same instructions.

Luke also chronicled the fact that, on occasion, Jesus invited an inner circle of three men to participate in an even deeper level of relationship with him. Separating themselves from the rest of the twelve, the other disciples, and the crowds, Jesus often asked Peter, James, and John to pray with him in private. In the four Gospels, a number of these intimate prayer meetings were described. These times sometimes marked significant events in the life of Jesus and enduring memories in the lives of the members of the inner circle.

In the transfiguration, Luke 9:28-36, Jesus and his inner circle of friends climbed a mountain to find a quiet place to pray. Although Peter, James, and John were sleepy, they watched carefully as Jesus prayed. They had observed Jesus' prayers on other occasions, but on that night, what they witnessed a truly remarkable and mysterious moment. On that night, Jesus' prayers were so intense that that his appearance changed; his face and clothing glowed, creating a dazzling aura. Unexpectedly, Jesus was joined by two mysterious and glorious figures. Somehow, Peter, James, and John identified these figures as Moses and Elijah, the Law Giver and the Prophet, both heroes of the Jewish faith. Luke reported that the apostles overheard their conversation with Jesus, a conversation in which Moses and Elijah talked with Jesus about the culmination of his ministry in Jerusalem. Overwhelmed by this experience, Peter asked Jesus for permission to build dwellings for this unique trinity. Suddenly, a mysterious cloud covered the entire scene, causing terror in the hearts of the inner circle. From the cloud came a voice: "This is my Son, my Chosen; listen to him!" Then, as suddenly as it began, the cloud cleared and Jesus was alone with his friends.

Remarkably, the scriptures record that Peter, James, and John did not immediately share this experience with others. They kept silent. Perhaps they were too overwhelmed by the mystery of the moment to understand or to appreciate its significance. Nonetheless, this experience was a defining moment shared by Jesus and his inner circle. In prayer and through divine revelation, Jesus found affirmation and encouragement for his mission and ministry. In their openness to experience the intimacy and the mystery of that moment, the inner circle of apostles began to develop a deeper understanding of and appreciation for their teacher, his work, and ultimately, their own ministry.

Intimacy and Contemporary Discipleship

As demonstrated throughout the Gospel of Luke, Jesus chose to live in intimate relationship with the people with whom he ministered. He established a hospitable community of disciples, friends, and supporters as he proclaimed the Kingdom of God. He ministered to these people and they, in turned, ministered to him and to his needs. When they were ready, Jesus selected members of this band of brothers and sisters with whom he shared his mission and demonstrated the character of the disciple—complete dependence on God. Finally, Jesus shared intimate moments of prayer and mysterious epiphanies with his inner circle of apostles.

In our contemporary context, Jesus still invites his disciples to live in intimate relationship with him. I am regularly reminded of the intimate nature of this relationship by a t-shirt often worn by "Joe," one of own undergraduate students at Campbell University. On the chest of his simple, black shirt is the phrase, "I'm in Love with a Man…" On the back of the shirt are the words, "Jesus Christ." As a self-professed postmodern, "Joe" wears this shirt around our conservative, evangelical university for its "shock value." But the truth contained in his t-shirt theology cannot be denied. The call to follow is a call to intimacy established in ongoing relationship. As contemporary disciples, we are called to fall "truly, madly, and deeply" in love with Jesus Christ. As we develop this level of intimate relationship, we will take on the character of disciple and share his mission to our lost and hurting world.

An Affirmation of Faith: Jesus Calls Us Each to Follow
Jesus calls us each to follow, Learn of Him and make Him know,
Calls us each our lives to offer serving those who are His own.
As we strive to heed the Savior, His commission to fulfill,
May we find in Christ our Center That we might do God's will.

—Verse 1 of the Campbell University
Divinity School Hymn,
words by Steven R. Harmon,
used with permission.

Resource Page

In Luke 4:38-41, 5:27-39, and 10:38-42, Jesus was invited to visit in the homes of some of his followers. Read these passages. Then, describe your impressions of Jesus' relationship with each of the people who opened their home to him.

_____

_____

_____

_____

_____

_____

In Luke 5:1-11, Jesus invited three of his followers to leave their profession to pursue a new vocation. Read the passage and describe the interaction between Simon and Jesus. Based on this passage, how would you characterize their relationship?

_____

_____

_____

_____

_____

_____

Firmly grounded in an intimate relationship with Jesus, all Christians are called to mission and ministry in the name of Christ. This calling is expressed in all aspects of our lives—in family, in community with other believers, with friends, and in our workplace. If these assumptions are accurate, in reality, all Christians live with the people with whom they minister. How might you respond this statement?

_____

_____

_____

_____

_____

_____

In Luke 9:1-6 and in 10:1-12, Jesus commissioned his disciples to share his ministry, proclaiming the Gospel and healing the sick. In their ministry, the disciples were challenged to model the character of a true disciple—total dependence on God for their basic needs. As a contemporary of disciple of Christ, describe one specific way that you have modeled dependence of God in your relationship with Christ.

_____

_____

_____

_____

_____

_____

Recall a personal experience in which you shared a remarkable sense of God's presence with intimate, Christian friends. In the space below, record that experience and speculate on why was that experience is so meaningful to you.

_____

_____

_____

_____

_____

_____

On a scale of 1 to 10, with 1 as "very distant" and 10 as "very intimate," how would you describe your relationship with Jesus Christ at this point in time? What factors lead you to this assessment? Based on this lesson, list at least one specific way in which you can develop a more intimate relationship with Jesus Christ.

_____

_____

_____

_____

_____

_____

Character Developed Through Ministry with Marginalized People

Focal Passage: Luke 19:1-10

Central Truth of the Session

In the Gospel of Luke, Jesus demonstrated radical inclusiveness as he ministered to persons on the margins of society. His unconditional acceptance of these people produced healing and restoration.

Religious Leader, Insurrectionist, or Servant?

Before Jesus began his public ministry, he had to address several critical questions about his life, his work, and his future. What type of person had God called him to be? How would he face the temptation to be less than what God had called him to be? How would he define his mission in life? Where would he live and work? Who would be his closest friends? With what type of people would he associate?

Jesus could have chosen to live out his calling as a Jewish religious leader and teacher, working within the established faith system. If he had made this choice, he would have probably lived in Jerusalem and centered his work in the Temple. He would have associated with other prominent religious leaders—the chief priests, the scribes, the Pharisees, and the Sadducees. In this context, he would have spent his days debating the interpretation of Torah and challenging established religious beliefs and structures. This lifestyle would have been one valid way of living out his relationship with God.

Jesus might have chosen to become a political revolutionary and military leader. If he had made this choice, he could have, in all likelihood, attracted many followers, patriots intent on overthrowing the Roman armies of occupation. Hiding in the hills and desolate places, Jesus could have inspired and trained an army to march on

Jerusalem and to reestablish the Kingdom of David. Again, many expected this type of activity from God's Chosen One.

Obviously, Jesus chose a different path. In his inaugural sermon, Luke 4:16-19, Jesus declared that his ministry would focus on the poor, the captives, the blind, and the oppressed. Rather than living in Jerusalem, Jesus and his followers would walk from village to village, encountering people with all sorts of needs. Rather than debating theology or planning insurrection, Jesus would heal people who were hurting, comfort people who had experienced loss, and model a unique lifestyle for his disciples. Rather than spending most of his time with religious leaders or zealots, Jesus would openly associate with people who lived at the margins of acceptable society.

Exploring Biblical Truth: Radical Inclusiveness

A major theme in the Gospel of Luke is the racial inclusiveness of Jesus' ministry. This inclusiveness extended to:

- People with leprosy (5:12-16 and 17:11-19), people who were possessed by demons (4:31-37), people who were paralyzed (5:17-26), a man with a withered hand (6:6-10), and a man who was blind from birth (18:35-43).
- Children, who seemed to occupy a special place in Jesus' heart (18:15-17).
- Women, including a woman of questionable reputation (7:36-50) and a group of women who traveled with and ministered to Jesus and his disciples (8:2-3).
- Tax collectors and sinners, including one his disciples, Levi (Lk 5:27-32).
- A Roman officer who displayed remarkable faith (7:1-10).

His inclusiveness also extended to "the multitudes," crowds of people from all walks of life, who gathered around Jesus. Why were these people attracted to Jesus? Some wanted to be healed; others wanted to witness the miracles. Some were curious; others wanted to be fed. Some wanted to hear his teachings; others hoped that he was Messiah. From the Sermon on the Plain (Lk 6:17-49), to the Feeding of the 5000 (Lk 9:10-17, to the triumphant entry into Jerusalem (19:28-40), Jesus ministered to the "great, unwashed masses."

The focal passage of this session illustrates the radical inclusiveness of Jesus' ministry. This passage, found only in the Gospel of

Luke, tells the story of one of these questionable characters with whom Jesus chose to associate.

An Interpretative Paraphrase of the Passage: Living Up to Your Name

In Israel many years ago, a man and a woman rejoiced at the birth of a son. In accordance with Jewish tradition, the proud parents gathered with family and friends one week after his birth to dedicate their son to God. It was during this service of dedication that the father first announced his son's name. And what a name it was! In those days, a person's name held great significance. The name described the personality or character of the bearer, and these proud and hopeful parents had selected a very special name for their child. He was named Zacchaeus, which means "pure" or "righteous." As they assembled for the dedication, they were optimistic that he would "live up" to his name.

But something happened along the way, something that led Zacchaeus to disgrace his name. For whatever reason, Zacchaeus chose to follow a path of collaboration with the enemies of Israel, a path of dishonesty and greed. When Luke introduced his readers to the adult Zacchaeus, he had rejected his name, his people, and his God.

The story began in Jericho, an important city on the border of Judea, some fifteen miles northeast of Jerusalem. The city was a major center of agriculture and commerce on the north-south trade routes through Palestine. A constant flow of goods and produce made this a prosperous place to live and work, especially for a tax collector.

In first century Palestine, the process used to collect taxes was complicated and confusing. All personal and property taxes were collected directly by the Roman government, but customs duties on goods and produce were collected by private contractors. These contractors, also known as publicans, received no salary from the government. Roman law did allow them to collect all the taxes owed to Rome and then to charge any additional fees that they could collect. As you might suspect, the system provided unlimited opportunity for abuse and exploitation.

Over the years, Zacchaeus had learned this system well, so well that he was made a district tax manager for the Romans. He had used his skills to amass great wealth, presumably through the unfair collection of taxes. As the chief tax collector in the prosperous town of Jericho, he could have an almost unlimited income of his own, with additional monies coming in from a number of subordinate collectors responsible to him. In short, Zacchaeus was at the top of a tax pyramid scheme.

His great wealth came at a costly price. He was a man without a people. On one hand, even though he worked loyally for the Roman government, he was still a Jew and was, therefore, unacceptable in Roman social circles. On the other hand, his own people probably considered him both a traitor and a thief. His contact with the Romans and his sins against God and his fellow Jews would have caused him to be excluded from the synagogue and ostracized from all decent Jewish folks. In all probability, Zacchaeus was the most notorious—and marginalized—citizen of Jericho.

In the midst of his notoriety and isolation, the scriptures indicated that Zacchaeus heard that Jesus was coming through town. No one knows exactly what Zacchaeus knew about Jesus or why he chose to see him. Perhaps it was curiosity; maybe it was conscience. For whatever reason, Zacchaeus made a special effort to see the teacher from Galilee. To venture out into a crowd was great risk for Zacchaeus; in a large public gathering, the hated tax collector might come to bodily harm. Beyond this threat of danger, Zacchaeus could not be sure that he would see Jesus as he passed because he was "short of stature." Yet, he ventured out into the crowd and found a solution to his problem. Zacchaeus climbed into the low-hanging, broad branches of a sycamore tree. Though not the safest place for a man so despised by the public, the diminutive Zacchaeus perched in the foliage of the tree and waited for a glimpse of Jesus.

As the crowds swayed past the sycamore tree, Jesus first did the unexpected. In the midst of an ocean of people, all vying for his attention, Jesus paused to look up into the tree! When he spotted Zacchaeus, he did the unspeakable. Jesus invited himself to dinner: "Zacchaeus, hurry and come down; for I must stay at your house today."

In that instant, at that moment of invitation, what a mix of thoughts and feelings must have flooded over Zacchaeus. He may have thought, "Who is this Jesus? No Jew would have anything to do with me. After all, I am a sinner. No one would greet me or extend the basic courtesies to me, much less offer warmth and friendship. Then along comes this man who speaks to me without censure, without condition. In front of all the people he declares that he is coming to my house." Zacchaeus hurried down the tree and eagerly responded to the invitation to go (or possibly to come) home.

The happy scene was interrupted by the response of the crowds. The people murmured in disbelief. They grumble to Jesus; "Don't you know who this is? Don't you know what he does for a living? No self-respecting Jewish person would even acknowledge this man, let alone go to his house. This man is a sinner." In these circumstances, Jesus' acceptance of the despised Zacchaeus constituted a bold, public act. But where the welfare of a person was at stake, Jesus ignored all taboos. Not only did he recognize and speak to Zacchaeus, but he chose to make the house of an unclean man his rest stop, thereby shocking all the religious people in the crowd.

The shock is compounded by the fact that, to this point in the story, Zacchaeus had not publicly confessed his transgressions. He had not shown any evidence that he had repented of his sinful actions. And yet, Jesus' acceptance of Zacchaeus was public and unconditional. At no time had Jesus lectured Zacchaeus about his profession or his past sins. He did not say, "If you will give up your job and stop doing the things that make it costly for me to associate with you, I will go to your house." Jesus said publicly, "Zacchaeus, you come down, for I'm going to your house today."

The impact of unconditional acceptance by Jesus began a transformation in the life and character of Zacchaeus. The first sign of this transformation was a radical change in his attitude toward wealth. We find this new attitude described in Luke 19:8-10. For some reason, many contemporary readers of the Gospel operate under the mistaken impression that the conversation recorded in these verses occurred at Zacchaeus' house later that evening. They believe that somehow, Jesus required the tax collector to demonstrate a new attitude about money before salvation could be pronounced. This was not the case, however. Zacchaeus did not begin the path toward transformation by trying to negotiate a contract with Jesus in the privacy of his dining room. His path to a new life began when he climbed out of that tree. In verse 8, Zacchaeus stood there on the street, in the midst of a crowd of people whom he had cheated, and confessed his faith in the only way that he knew how.

Responding to Jesus' offer of unconditional acceptance and to the transformation already at work in his life, it was Zacchaeus' turn to do the unexpected. According to the letter of Jewish law, he was only required to pay back the original amount that he had extorted, plus a 20% penalty. But Zacchaeus went beyond accepted conventions; he first promised to give half of his considerable fortune to the poor. Then, he swore to give back 400% to the other taxpayers! Greed turned to extravagant generosity. In response to his generosity, Jesus offered words of blessing: "Today, salvation has come to this house, because Zacchaeus too is a son of Abraham. For the Son of Man has come to seek and to save the lost." Once a scoundrel by his own choosing, Zacchaeus began to live up to his name.

(For more information, see Tolbert, 146-47; Miller, 77-81.)

Unconditional Acceptance

When Jesus called the tax collector Levi to follow him as a disciple, Levi responded by inviting Jesus to his house for a meal. Other tax collectors and notorious sinners attended the dinner. When the Pharisees and their scribes complained to Jesus' disciples about the guest list, Jesus responded, "Those who are well have no need of a physician, but those who are sick; I have come to call not the righteous but sinners to repentance" (Lk 5:31).

As reported in the Luke's Gospel, Jesus chose to associate with the people who were notorious and marginalized. Abandoning social and religious conventions, Jesus modeled a rare character trait for his followers: *unconditional acceptance*. Jesus was not naïve regarding the behaviors and attitudes of the people with whom he chose to minister. He readily acknowledged the fact that they were sinners in need of repentance. But repentance was not a precondition for relationship with Jesus. Rather, Jesus' unconditional acceptance was the beginning point for repentance and, ultimately, transformation. Something drew Zacchaeus to risk the retribution of his neighbors in order to see Jesus. Something completely unexpected happened when Jesus paused to publicly invite himself to dinner at the home of the tax collector. In this simple act of unconditional acceptance, Zacchaeus began a life-long process of healing and restoration. It took no public confession or act of devotion—it was literally as simple as falling out of a sycamore tree.

Mirrors of Potential

Unconditional acceptance was one important aspect of Jesus' interaction with Zacchaeus. In his book, *Your Golden Shadow: Discovering and Fulfilling Your Undeveloped Self*, William Miller provides an additional commentary on this passage and suggests another critical dynamic in the story. Miller asserts that, in his associations with the infamous and insignificant, Jesus possessed the rare ability to see people both as they are *and* as God intended them to be. In short, Miller believes that Jesus could see the potential of an individual, i.e. their "golden shadow," and invite them to live into that potential (Miller, 78-81). This idea is supported by an illustration found in *The Interpreter's Bible* commentary series. In a sermon entitled, "The Mirror," Lloyd Douglas composed a fictional conversation between Jesus and Zacchaeus. At the end of the exciting day described in Luke 19:1-10, Lloyd conjectured that Jesus turned to Zacchaeus and asked him why he had been so eager to accept his invitation to transformation. "Zacchaeus," said the carpenter gently, "what did you see that made you desire this peace?" "Good master, I saw, mirrored in your eyes, the face of the Zacchaeus I was meant to be" (Douglas, 74)! Because he clearly understood himself and his own unique relationship with God, Jesus was able to be a mirror for others to explore their own personhood and relationship with God.

Resource Page

In this lesson, a number of passages were cited to support the radical inclusiveness of Jesus' ministry. Read each passage cited in that section. As you read, describe your understanding of Jesus' interaction with each of the following groups:

People with illnesses
People who were grieving
Children
Women
Notorious sinners
A Roman soldier

_____

_____

_____

_____

_____

_____

Have you experienced a relationship in which another person offered you unconditional acceptance as described in this passage? Have you experience a relationship in which you have offered unconditional acceptance to another person? If so, describe these experiences in the space below.

In the contemporary context, what types of people are considered to be notorious and marginalized? Identify at least one specific example of a time when you, as an individual, or your church, as a body of believers, have ministered with the type of people

---

Have you experienced a relationship in which another person mirrored your potential and challenged you to live into that potential? Have you experienced a relationship in which you have mirrored the potential of another person and challenged that person to live into that potential? If so, describe these experiences in the space below.

7

Character Tempered
Through Confrontation

Focal Passage: Luke 14:1-14

Central Truth of the Session

In the Gospel of Luke, the life, ministry, and teachings of Jesus challenged the conventional religious beliefs and practices of the Jewish religious leaders. This posture led to escalating levels of conflict with these leaders. In these confrontations, Jesus clearly contrasted the character of the religious leaders and the character of a true disciple.

Administration or Leadership?

As an assistant professor of Christian Education in a divinity school, I teach basic principles of church administration and congregational leadership in many of my courses. Occasionally, I use the following exercise to help my students distinguish between these two areas of congregational ministry.

I begin the discussion with the following statement: "By definition, an administrator is called to maintain and to defend the status quo; a leader is called to challenge the status quo and to offer a clear vision the future." Then I asked, "Do you agree or disagree with this statement? Why or why not?" After a few minutes of discussion, I say, "For the sake of argument, let's agree that the statement is accurate. Given these two options—administrator or leader—what do you believe is the role of a minister in the congregational context?" Typically, the majority of the students in the class state their belief that a minister should be a leader. Next, I ask those students who are currently working in a church the following question: "Now that you are actually ministering in a congregational context, day in and day out, do you function more as an administrator or a leader?" Predictability, the majority of the members of the class say that they actually function as administrators.

This exercise is designed to begin a deeper discussion of the expectations of and tensions associated with our dual calling. On one hand, ministers of the Gospel are called to defend the beliefs and practices of the Christian faith and of the church. At the same time, ministers are also called to challenge many of these beliefs and practices in favor of a clearer vision of the Kingdom of God and a more faithful practice of Christian discipleship.

Exploring Biblical Truth: A Leader with Authority

In the passages selected for this session, the dynamics associated with these expectations and tensions are also at work in Luke's presentation of the Gospel story. In these passages, we find a conflict brewing between the established religious leaders, the self-proclaimed administrators of the Jewish faith, and Jesus. Based on his understanding of his unique relationship with God, Jesus was a leader with authority. Jesus challenged his disciples and these religious leaders to participate in a broader vision of the Kingdom of God. As this conflict developed, Jesus also took many opportunities to contrast the character of these religious leaders with the character of the true disciple.

As described in previous sessions in this study, Jesus began his public ministry with a clear understanding of who he was in relationship to God. This understanding was affirmed at his baptism. Based on the firm foundation of this unique relationship, Jesus then publicly declared his mission in life—proclaiming the Kingdom of God and working among the poor, the captives, the blind, and the oppressed. Eventually, Jesus began to live out his mission and ministry by traveling, teaching, and healing.

As news of his authoritative teaching and miraculous healings spread, the established religious leaders were at first curious about the man from Galilee. A careful reading of the Gospel of Luke showed that Jesus had ongoing contact with these leaders. Since Jesus regularly attended and taught in synagogues, he was acquainted with local religious leaders. In fact, Luke reported that Jarius, a man identified as a leader of a local synagogue, asked Jesus to come to his house in order to heal his sick daughter. When the girl died before they arrived at the house, Jesus comforted the parents and brought her back to life (See Lk 8:40-56). For whatever reason, "Pharisees and teachers of the law" were often present as Jesus taught and healed the sick (as in Lk 5:17-26) and dined with his disciples and their friends (as in Lk 5:27-32). Several times, prominent Pharisees actually invited Jesus into their homes for a meal (See Lk 7:36-50 and the focal passage). These encounters seem to indicate that, at least at first, the religious leaders viewed Jesus with wonder and curiosity, if not with a bit of suspicion.

Serious conflict was inevitable when Jesus began to publicly claim that his unique relationship with God was the basis for his authoritative teaching, his disregard of Sabbath restrictions, and his ability to heal the sick and injured. In his teaching ministry, Jesus shared simple stories and parables that indirectly questioned the character and behavior of the religious leaders. Declaring himself "the Son of Man" and "the Lord of the Sabbath," Jesus regularly set aside Sabbath restrictions in order to meet the needs of the sick. In his healing ministry, Jesus claimed and demonstrated the authority to forgive sins. This claim of authority became the critical issue in the conflict. With their role as the final authority on all matters of faith threatened by Jesus' claims of authority, the religious leaders were angry and righteously indignant. They privately accused Jesus of blasphemy and conspired to collect as much evidence as possible to support this accusation.

As the religious leaders conspired against him, Jesus challenged the character, attitude, and practices of these leaders in very public contexts. At times, Jesus was very direct in his criticisms.

In Luke 11:37-54, at a dinner in the home of Pharisee, his host criticized Jesus because he did not ritually wash his hands before the meal. In some of the harshest words recorded in the Gospel of Luke, Jesus blasted the Pharisees and lawyers for their misplaced priorities in the practice of their faith.

In Luke 19:45-48, Jesus directly challenged the authority of the religious leaders in Jerusalem when he drove merchants out of the Temple. Then, the entire 20th chapter of the Gospel described a series of confrontations between Jesus and various religious leaders over the source of his authority and his interpretation of scripture and religious practice.

At other times, Jesus chose to take a less direct approach. In these instances, he used parables to criticize the character of the religious leaders and to describe the character of the true disciple. The focal passage in this session described one of these occasions.

An Interpretive Paraphrase: The Inhospitable Dinner Guest

In Luke 14:1-24, Jesus was invited to a Sabbath meal at the house of an unidentified leader of the Pharisees. It was a common practice to gather after services in the synagogue for special celebrations and feasting. The meal would have been prepared on Friday evening (in anticipation of work restrictions associated with the Sabbath) and then served the next day to family, friends, and invited guests. At times, these meals were community events; at the discretion of the host, people from the town or village might be allowed to enter and leave the festivities as they pleased.

Under ordinary circumstances, an invitation of this nature would hold mutual benefit for both the host and an honored guest. The host could boast that he had a well-known and much sought-after guest in his home. The guest could boast that he had a special invitation from a prominent religious leader to attend a function that included many rich and prominent people. The Gospel recorded that this particular celebrative meal was, however, not conducted under ordinary circumstances. The intent of the invitation was clear; the Pharisees wanted to watch Jesus closely during the event. The implication was that they hoped to catch Jesus in some violation of Jewish law or tradition.

The host and his guests did not have to wait long for the opportunity for a violation to present itself. Before the meal began, a sick man wandered into the festivities. The man was described as having dropsy, a disorder of the heart or kidneys that caused the retention of excess body fluids. By this point in his ministry, Jesus had been presented with this same situation on numerous occasions. In the presence of the lawyers and the Pharisees, the defenders of tradition, Jesus had to answer a question: should he meet the physical needs of an individual or should he observe a strict interpretation of the Sabbath laws? In every instance reported in the Gospels, Jesus chose the needs of the individual over the rules of the Sabbath.

In this instance, before he healed the man, he did due diligence; he intentionally sought the expert opinion of his hosts, the religious professionals. In 14:3 he asked, "Is it lawful to cure people on the Sabbath, or not?" While the authorities responded with awkward silence, Jesus responded in compassion. The scriptures report that he "took the man," possibly in an embrace, healed him, and sent him on his way. In exasperation, Jesus then tried to describe a practical situation in which the religious leaders might choose to ignore Sabbath work restrictions. In effect, he asked, "Surely you would have the compassion to get your child or your ox out of a well on the Sabbath?" Again the authorities responded with silence.

At this point in the evening, the guests began to assemble in the dining area. Protocol and etiquette suggested a seating chart. Close friends and most esteemed guests were seated closest to the host, while persons of casual acquaintance or of lower social station were often seated at some distance from the host and his intimates. On this night, Jesus could not help but notice that many of the guests were jockeying for a place of honor. In response to this struggle for position, Jesus told a parable.

In his account of the Gospel, Luke was very careful to identify this teaching as a parable, a story about an everyday situation that pointed to a deeper truth. Jesus did not presume to give the scribes and Pharisees lessons in protocol and etiquette; they were the masters of these matters. Instead, Jesus sought to illustrate deeper truths about humility. The first part of the parable parodied the behavior and the attitude that Jesus had just witnessed in the room—guests at a wedding banquet wrongly assuming that they were the most important people at the event. Their presumption led to their humiliation when, in front of the other guests, they were asked to move from the seats of honor to the bottom of the table. The second part of the parable explained the behavior and the attitude of the true disciple. One should humbly assume the lowest place and be pleasantly surprised when, in front of everyone, the host insists that his humble guest be seated in a place of honor. Jesus concluded the parable with a paradoxical conclusion about humility and exaltation.

At this point, Jesus made another observation about his host and his guests. The scriptures implied that the people in attendance at this dinner were, like their host, prominent and powerful. In what had to be an embarrassing moment, Jesus critiqued the host for his selection of guests by sharing a second parable. This parable contrasted conventional hospitality with true hospitality. Conventional hospitality, as practiced by the host, issued invitations to family, friends, and wealth neighbors in hopes of being invited to their fabulous parties. True hospitality, as demonstrated in the radical inclusiveness of Jesus' ministry, invited the most unlikely people to the party specifically because they would be unable to repay the favor. Conventional hospitality satisfied the need for an immediate reciprocity; true hospitality held a different set of rewards.

Perhaps to ease the mounting tension caused by Jesus' comments, one of the other guests said, "Blessed is anyone who will eat bread in the kingdom of God!" Many commentators judged this statement to be a pious platitude uttered by a man who is smugly certain that he will definitely receive an invitation to that dinner! Jesus reinterpreted his comment with a third parable.

The parable of the Great Dinner, recorded in Luke 14:16-23, told the story of a person who had issued formal invitations to an extended period of feasting. Many people were invited and all indicated that they would attend. When the host sent his servant to collect his guests for the festivities, each had changed his or her mind. Politely, they made excuses to the servant. One had to check out a real estate investment. A second had to test the pulling capacity of new yoke of oxen. A third had pressing family obligations. When the servant returned to his master with the news, the host was angry, but determined. He commissioned his servant to "Go out at once into the streets and lanes of the town and bring in the poor, the crippled, the blind, and the lame" (See Lk 14:21b). The servant did as he was told, returning with the news that there was still room at the party. The host then instructed the servant to go back out and take all steps necessary to insure that all the people surprised by this unexpected invitation would know, beyond a shadow of a doubt, that they were indeed welcomed at the festivities.

As Jesus spoke this parable, some of the dinner guests may have recognized themselves in the story. They probably understood that Jesus equated those who first received and then rejected the invitations with the Pharisees. Most likely, they did not agree the Jesus' characterization of these unresponsive guests. The fact that the marginalized and the unexpected, perhaps even the Gentiles, would replace them in the heavenly banquet was probably beyond their comprehensive.

With the parable concluded, Jesus turned his attention back to his host and his fellow guests. Speaking now in first person, Jesus warned that an invitation to the banquet was not enough; only those who demonstrated the proper response at the decisive moment would participate in "my banquet." With this remark, Luke's account of this dinner party ended.

(For more information, see Tolbert, 118-21; Gilmour, 251-59.)

A Difference in Character

From the beginning, the life and ministry of Jesus challenged the conventional religious beliefs and practices of the Jewish religious leaders. On a deeper level, Jesus also questioned their character. In the focal passage of this session, the contrast between the character of the religious leaders and the character of a true disciple was clear:

- While the religious leaders meticulously observed the letter of the Jewish law, Jesus compassionately met the needs of the sick.
- Position and prestige were the order of the day when the religious leaders gathered; genuine humility was the mark of the true disciple.
- The religious leaders practiced hospitality based on reciprocity; the true disciple practiced hospitality based on radical inclusiveness, with no expectation of repayment.
- Unlike the religious leaders of the day, the true disciple has a proper sense of priority; the affairs of this age will not stop the disciple from accepting Jesus' invitation to participate in the Kingdom of God (Tolbert 120-21).

Resource Page

Luke 5:17-26, 5:27-32, 7:36-50, and 8:40-56 document Jesus' ongoing contact with religious leaders during the early stages of his ministry. Read each passage and describe your understanding of Jesus' relationship with the religious leaders in that passage.

In your own words, describe how Jesus' understanding of his unique relationship with God led to his confrontations with the religious leaders.

_____

_____

_____

_____

_____

_____

In Luke 14:4a, the Pharisees are silent when Jesus asked them about the legality of healing on the Sabbath. Why do think they chose not to respond?

_____

_____

_____

_____

_____

_____

_____

Based on your reading of Luke 14:7-11, how should a contemporary disciple of Jesus Christ embody the character trait of humility?

_____

_____

_____

_____

_____

_____

Based on your reading of Luke 14:12-14, how should a contemporary disciple of Jesus Christ embody the character trait of hospitality?

_____

_____

_____

_____

_____

_____

What does your reading of Luke 14:15-34 tell you about the priorities of a contemporary disciple of Jesus Christ?

_____

_____

_____

_____

_____

Character Developed Through Resources Used Ambitiously and Creatively

Focal Passage: Luke 16:1-9

Central Truth of the Session

In the parable of the Unjust Steward, Jesus introduced a very unlikely role model for Christian discipleship and conveyed a surprising truth about the creative use of all resources on behalf of the Kingdom of God.

Contemporary Examples of Christian Stewardship?

What do Franklin Roosevelt, Donald Trump, Bill Gates, and a character in one of Jesus' parables have in common? According to the focal passage of this lesson, each one of these entrepreneurs can be a role model for Christian discipleship and an example of service to the Kingdom of God. If you find this hard to believe, read on!

Exploring Biblical Truth: Wealth and Poverty

In the Gospel of Luke, Jesus challenged his followers to adopt a radically different understanding of finances, wealth, and the accumulation of possessions.

At a time when the popular theology held that wealth and abundance of possessions were sure signs of God's special blessings, Luke focused on stories and teachings in which Jesus stated that God would lift up the poor and cast out the rich. (Refer to Luke 6:20-26.)

At a time when the average family labored many hours each day just to meet their basic physical needs, Jesus challenged his followers to depend completely on God and to seek God's Kingdom. (Refer to Lk 12:13-31.)

When Jesus commissioned his disciples, he sent them into the world empty-handed, and they wanted for nothing. (Refer to Lk 9:1-6, 10:1-2, and 22:35-38.)

When a rich ruler, a man who meticulously observed the Jewish laws and traditions, came with questions, Jesus required him to divest his money before he could invest in the Kingdom. As the ruler walked away from the deal, Jesus' response confounded his own disciples. (Refer to Lk 18:18-30.)

When his critics attempted to trap him in a question about taxes paid to the occupying Roman government, Jesus used the opportunity to teach a deeper truth. (Refer to Lk 20:20-26.)

Instead of affirming the gift of a wealthy man, a gift offered with much pomp and circumstance, Jesus lavishly praised the quiet, sacrificial gift of the widow's mite. (Refer to Lk 21:1-4.)

In each of these examples, Jesus directly confronted conventional wisdom regarding finances, wealth, and the accumulation of possessions. In the focal text for this session, Jesus turned conventional wisdom "on its head" and then spun it around. In this passage, found only in the Luke's Gospel, Jesus introduced his followers to a memorable character, the Unjust Steward, and revealed a surprising truth about the nature of discipleship and the wise use of resources.

Setting the Context of the Passage

In the 15th chapter of Luke, Jesus addressed a crowd that included Pharisees, publicans, and his disciples. In this case, the word "disciples" does not specifically refer to the twelve, but rather to the followers of Jesus, in general. Then, at the beginning of chapter 16, Jesus turned his attention to his followers, with the rest of the group listening in the background, overhearing his conversation.

An Interpretive Paraphrase of the Passage: Surprising Stewardship

In this story, Jesus introduced his hearers to a wealthy landowner, a man who had so many possessions that he required the services of a manager, or steward. Typically, such a steward would have been responsible for the operation of a large country estate while the owner lived in a town or city. Somehow, the landowner heard charges that his steward was less than forthright in the management of properties entrusted to him. The owner confronted his steward with these accusations. He then demanded a full account of all business transactions in order to make a judgment about these accusations. If the charges were true, the steward would lose his job.

It is very interesting to note that the steward made no formal statement of guilt or innocence to his boss. Those folks listening to the story, however, were given a unique perspective into the thoughts of the accused, leaving no doubt that the steward was guilty as charged. He was positive that the results of the investigation will lead to his dismissal. In light of this fact, he pondered his future. While dishonest in his business dealings, the steward was brutally honest in his self-assessment. He considered himself too weak to do manual labor and too proud to beg. The steward faced a true dilemma.

In a sudden burst of insight, the intrepid manager remembered that, at least for the present, he still possessed the power and authority of the stewardship, and that this power and authority could be used to provide for his future well-being. The steward had an ingenious idea. He developed a plan through which his master's debtors would feel a sense of obligation to him. Hopefully, his generosity would lead to their hospitality in the long, hard days ahead. He seized the initiative.

The steward called his master's debtors to him, first as a group, then in private conferences. The parable contained only two examples of these conversations; others were implied. In the first meeting, the steward requested a credit report and found that the account included 100 liquid measures of oil. The steward then produced the original contract, probably in the debtor's own handwriting. The contract was a record of the amount of raw material that the debtor had to produce within a specified period of time as payment for property rental. The debtor was told to quickly alter the numbers, in this case, to change only one Aramaic letter, in order to cut the debt in half. In this fashion, the debtor became a part of the plot, hopefully insuring his silence. The debtor would then owe our audacious steward a secret favor. Discovered or not, the action of the steward was legally binding until the steward was officially terminated by the landowner. A second debtor was offered the same deal, with similar results. In a short period, the steward made many "future friends."

All good things must come to an end, however. Again, some unidentified source informed the landowner of the steward's dishonest activities. Here, the story took an unexpected twist. The rich owner actually commended his steward for the shrewd methods that he used to address the situation. The parable ended there, leaving Jesus' hearers to speculate on the ultimate fate of the steward.

It was at this point that Jesus began his first and primary commentary on the parable. He also revealed a surprising truth from the story. The second half of verse 8 was an indictment of the "sons of light," probably a reference to the followers of Jesus who are listening to the parable, with regard to their stewardship of the Kingdom of God on this earth. Jesus stated that a lesson should be learned from the "sons of darkness," maybe a reference to the Pharisees and publicans listening in on the conversation, typified by the unjust steward of the story. These persons were obsessed with worldly pursuits, both religious and financial. They were shrewd and resourceful, using their personal resources (time, talents, abilities, and finances) to advance their position in this world. Jesus chided his followers, suggesting that they follow the example of these "sons of darkness." Jesus implied that his followers should use all of their personal resources as ambitiously and creatively as the "sons of darkness," but to achieve a higher purpose, that is, participation in the Kingdom of God. If the followers of Christ dedicated as much creative thinking and energy to the tasks of the Kingdom as the unjust steward did to provide for his own future, then the world would be a very different, and a better, place.

Finally, an additional and secondary commentary was offered in verse 9. Jesus told his disciples that each should properly use worldly substance, the "mammon of unrighteousness," to initiate friendships. This philanthropic use of earthly riches would then lead to long-term reward. The passage could be paraphrased, "Use your personal resources and material possessions wisely, making friends for yourselves, so that, in the day when these worldly resources fail, you may reap the benefit of these friendships, just as the steward used his control of resources to make friends for himself."

(For more information, see Tolbert, 127-29; Gilmour, 280-86.)

An Entrepreneurial Character

Given this intriguing story and Jesus' surprising interpretation of it, you may now see how Franklin, Donald, and Bill can serve as role models for Christian discipleship and examples of service to the Kingdom of God.

Whether or not you agree with his political philosophy, Franklin Roosevelt used all of his resources—his family name, his family fortune, his personal charm, and his ruthless political skills—to be elected to four terms as President, to guide the nation through of the Great Depression, and to lead the country during World War II. Capitalizing on the economic climate of the 1980s, Donald Trump aggressively dedicated all of his personal resources and skills to promote his own image and to create a real estate empire. As chronicled in the PBS series, *The Revenge of the Nerds*, Bill Gates dropped out of a prestigious college, began tinkering with computers in a garage, surrounded himself with an interesting group of other techno-heads, spent endless hours writing and de-bugging innovative computer programs, and eventually became one of the richest people in the history of the world.

Each of these men displayed a single-minded focus, a wealth of creativity, and an entrepreneurial spirit in the accumulation of worldly gains—power, position, public recognition, and money. In his commentary on the parable, Jesus commended these qualities, if not the goals toward which these qualities were directed. In fact, Jesus mildly chided his own followers for their lack of drive, ingenuity, and shrewdness in their stewardship of the Kingdom of God.

What might happen if we, as contemporary followers of Jesus Christ, invested ourselves in the work of the Kingdom of God with the same resourcefulness that these three men invested themselves in their personal ambitions?

The parable of the Unjust Steward challenged all followers of Jesus Christ to exhibit the character traits of ambition and creativity and to use these traits with an entrepreneurial spirit on behalf of the Kingdom of God. All Christians are counseled to use their time, abilities, and resources to serve and to minister with the same enthusiasm and effort that worldly people use their assets to pursue worldly gains. So, as you seek to be a more committed disciple of Jesus Christ, learn from Franklin, Donald, Bill, and the Unjust Steward!

Resource Page

Throughout the Gospel of Luke, Jesus offered unconventional financial advice to his first century listeners. Based on the following scriptures, speculate on what advice Jesus might give to the following contemporary persons:

A minister who preaches a gospel of health and wealth. (Lk 6:20-26)

A working-class Christian family who struggles to make ends meet. (Lk 12:13-31)

A Christian who cheatings on his or her taxes. (Lk 20:20-26)

A Christian who does not tithe. (Lk 21:1-4)

_____

_____

_____

_____

_____

In Luke 16:8-9, Jesus provided his assessment of the activities of the unjust steward. In the space below, paraphrase Jesus' understanding of these activities. What is your personal assessment of the unjust steward?

_____

_____

_____

_____

_____

On a scale of 1 to 10, with 1 as "not creative at all" and 10 as "very creative," how would you describe your uses of financial resources on behalf of the Kingdom of God? What factors lead you to this assessment?

_____

_____

_____

_____

_____

Based on this lesson, list at least one specific way in which you can be more creative in your financial stewardship.

_____

_____

_____

_____

_____

_____

On a scale of 1 to 10, with 1 as "not creative at all" and 10 as "very creative," how would you describe your uses of other resources (time, talents, gifts, passions, etc.) on behalf of the Kingdom of God? What factors lead you to this assessment?

_____

_____

_____

_____

_____

_____

Based on this lesson, list at least one specific way in which you can be more creative in your overall stewardship.

_____

_____

_____

_____

_____

_____

Character Tested by Consequences

Focal Passages: Luke 9:18-22; 9:37-45;
18:31-34; 9:23-27; 9:57-62; and14:25-35

Central Truth of the Session

Early in his ministry, Jesus recognized the ultimate consequences of
his decision to announce his unique relationship with God, i.e., his
sonship, and to conduct his ministry of teaching and healing based
on the authority of that relationship. In the Gospel of Luke, the
specter of these consequences cast a long shadow on his public life
and ministry. Nonetheless, in the face of conflict, suffering, and
death, Jesus was faithful to his understanding of his own mission
and calling. In the Gospel of Luke, Jesus also wanted his disciples to
understand the possible consequences of their decision to follow
him. In summary, the character of Jesus was tested by his understanding of the consequences of his identity and his ministry; the
same would be the case for the disciples of Jesus Christ.

"Bait and Switch" Discipleship

In his celebrated digest, *Harvey Penick's Little Red Book: Lessons and
Teachings from a Lifetime in Golf,* legendary golf coach Harvey
Penick shared anecdotal stories about many of the golfers he had
coached over the years. In one of these stories, Penick reflected on
the day he gave golf legend Ben Crenshaw his first lesson:

> Ben came to me when he was about eight years old. We
> cut off a 7-iron for him. I showed him a good grip, and
> we went outside.
>
> There was a green about 75 yards away. I asked Ben
> to tee up a ball and hit it onto the green. He did. Then

I said, "Now, let's go to the green and putt the ball into the hole."

"If you wanted it in the hole, why didn't you tell me the first time?" little Ben asked. (Penick, 138)

The dynamics and expectations at work in this brief sequence of events are quite amusing. As the experienced coach, Penick believed that his young apprentice was not capable of making a hole-in-one on his first day of lessons. As a favor to young Ben, he suggested a series of smaller, more easily achieved steps that would ultimately lead to the final goal. Penick's coaching experience and thoughtfulness were greeted with disdain. With youthful enthusiasm, tempered by naivety and arrogance, the young Crenshaw chided his famous coach for not describing the ultimate objective that he would be expected to achieve.

Unfortunately, similar dynamics and expectations may be at work with regard to issues of conversion and discipleship in some conservative evangelical churches. One of the major strengths of the evangelical movement is the heartfelt passion to share the Gospel in such a way that all persons may come to a saving knowledge of Jesus Christ as Savior and Lord. Make no mistake: this is an admirable goal. To achieve this end, however, many pastors and evangelists have divided this goal into a two-step process: conversion followed by discipleship. As experienced spiritual leaders, these ministers and evangelists realize that the ultimate demands of true Christian discipleship may be too much for an immature seeker to understand and to embrace fully. So they preach a gospel that places the *primary* emphasis on the need for Jesus Christ as Savior. Initially ignoring or severely deemphasizing the true cost of mature discipleship, their message is, "Do you love Jesus? Do you want to spend eternity with him and avoid eternal punishment? Then all you have to do is pray The Sinner's Prayer and you will be saved." Attracted by the wonderful simplicity of this message, many persons have made their "public profession of faith," proclaiming Jesus as *Savior*. Then, driven by a fervent desire to continue to share the gospel with other lost persons, these conservative evangelical leaders return to the work of making more converts. They assume, sometimes in error, that Christian educators and other church leaders will challenge these new Christians to address the second part of the process: becoming a mature Christian disciple who is able to confess that "Jesus is *Lord*."

The demands and consequences of mature Christian discipleship can be difficult even for an experienced Christian. For a new convert who has been led to Christ via the "Roman Road," the implications of living into the confession, "Jesus is Lord," can be overwhelming. When confronted with the ultimate demands of Christian discipleship—the radical transformation of character, values, and behaviors—some new converts simply choose not "to make Jesus Lord." They reason, "My sins have been forgiven and I will go to heaven when I die. I am a good member of my church. That's enough." Other converts question the judgment of their spiritual leaders, the persons who led them to Christ. Like little Ben Crenshaw in his first golf lesson, these folks say, "Why didn't someone tell me what was really expected of me before I made this decision?" Sadly, other Roman Road converts simply fall away from their initial commitment and from the church.

We can take heart in the fact that, ultimately, Ben Crenshaw became a great golfer, one of the best who ever played that sport. In similar fashion, we can also find comfort in the fact that many conservative evangelical Christian have eventually made Jesus Christ not only their Savior, but also the Lord of their lives. They have accepted the significant demands and ultimate consequences associated with living in relationship with Jesus Christ. But we must also be aware of the paralyzing effects of the "bait and switch" approach to conversion and discipleship described in this material. This approach to Christian commitment is not consistent with the pattern of discipleship model by Jesus in the Gospel of Luke. From the beginning of his ministry, Jesus carefully described the demands of discipleship to those persons whom he selected to follow him. Further, when potential converts came to Jesus and volunteered to follow him, Jesus used powerful and disturbing images to describe the possible consequences of Christian commitment, both for himself and for his true followers. The passages included in this session illustrate the fact that Jesus modeled and expected Christian character tested by the knowledge of ultimate consequences.

Three Predictions of Death and Resurrection

At some critical point in his life, either prior to his public ministry or at some point during that ministry, Jesus first recognized the range of possible outcomes associated with his decision to announce his unique relationship with God and to perform his ministry of teaching and healing based on the authority of that relationship.

Scripture does not indicate a time when Jesus came to this realization. Did he always understand the possible implications of his decisions? Was this understanding revealed to him in a specific moment, at a particular place? Or did he come to this understanding over the course of time, in a process of discovery? One can only speculate on when this happened.

Based on a careful reading of the texts, however, the reader of the Gospel of Luke can make at least two informed assumptions about how Jesus came to understand some of the possible consequences of his declaration of identity and of his ministry.

First, Jesus probably anticipated adverse consequences based on his reading of the same Scripture that he used to develop his mission in life. As reported in the first two sessions of the study, Jesus identified with the messianic image of the suffering servant and used this image as a lens through which to understand the nature of his ministry. Consistent with the ideas developed in the Servant Poems (See Isaiah 42:1-4, 49:1-6, 50:4-11, and 52:13–53:12), Jesus anticipated a ministry based on self-sacrifice, humility, and compassion. Furthermore, based on these passages, he publicly declared his intention to associate with and minister to all types of people living on the margins of acceptable society. While these passages may have provided guidance in his choice of identity and ministry role, the concepts developed in these scriptures also pointed Jesus toward an indication of the suffering and humiliation that would be associated with his life and work. The fourth Servant Poem, Isaiah 52:13–53:12, was particularly graphic in its description of what would happen to the God's anointed:

- this person would be despised and rejected by others (v.3);
- he would carry the infirmities and diseases of other people (v.4);
- the anointed would be wounded and crushed on behalf of the people (v.5);
- he would be oppressed and afflicted, yet he would remain silent (v.7); and
- a perversion of justice would lead to his undeserved and untimely death (v.8).

While most contemporary biblical scholars do not believe that Jesus consulted Jewish Scriptures to *predict* his ultimate fate, the implications of the passages are clear: the Scriptures clearly assume that the one who chooses to live out the role of the servant will be misunderstood and will suffer. Jesus *chose* the role and, in turn, *accepted* the consequences of that role.

Second, Jesus probably anticipated the consequences of his decisions based on the response of the people to his declaration of sonship, his teaching, and his healing. On one hand, throughout his Gospel, Luke highlighted his belief that Jesus was well received by his disciples, by his friends, and by scores of ordinary people. These folks were amazed and fascinated with Jesus. Amazement was not a universal reaction, however. As noted in the third session of this study, the people in Jesus' hometown of Nazareth were angry about his inclusive interpretation of Scripture (See Lk 4:16-30). Furthermore, as noted in Sessions Four and Seven of this study, Jesus experienced growing hostilities with various groups of Jewish religious leaders. When Jesus claimed his sonship as the source of his authority for teaching and healing, these leaders believed that he had committed blasphemy against God. The punishment for blasphemy was death (See Lev 24:16) and the religious establishment in Jerusalem, working in conjunction with the Roman government, was authorized to carry out this punishment. Jesus knew that his challenging teaching and his conflict with scribes, Pharisees, Sadducees, and the priest could have dire consequences.

Regardless of when or how Jesus came to this conclusion, a careful reading of the Gospel According to Luke illustrated that Jesus clearly realized that suffering and death would be a consequence of his relationship to God and of his ministry. In faith, he also trusted that this death would be followed by resurrection. In fact, Luke reported three predictions of Jesus' death and subsequent resurrection.

In Luke 9:18-22, Jesus and his disciples were alone together in a time of prayer. In this context, Jesus asked his disciples for some feedback. First, he wanted to know how the crowds understood his identity. After a brief report, he then asked the disciples, "But who do you say that I am?" (See v.20). Peter affirmed the fact that Jesus was the "Messiah of God." Immediately after this affirmation of identify, Jesus sternly commanded his disciples not to share this knowledge with others. Then he predicted that "The Son of Man" would undergo suffering, would be rejected by the religious establishment, would be killed, and would be raised on the third day (See vv.21-22).

In Luke 9:37-45, in front of large crowd, a man pleaded for Jesus to heal his only son who was demon-possessed. In previous attempts, Jesus' disciples had been unable to cast out the evil spirit that haunted the young man. After rebuking the disciples and the crowd, Jesus cast out the demon, healed the son, and returned him to his father. They were all astounded "at the greatness of God" (See v.43). In the context of this triumph over evil, while everyone was still celebrating his work, Jesus turned to his disciples and predicted that "The Son of Man is going to be betrayed into human hands" (See v.44). Interestingly, the disciples were somehow kept from comprehending the meaning of this statement, yet no one dared to ask for clarification.

In all probability, Jesus realized that the suffering and death he anticipated would take place in the city of Jerusalem. As the seat of religious, military, and governmental authority in Palestine, Jerusalem would be the location in which he would experience the ultimate consequences of his relationship with God and of his ministry. Obviously, if Jesus had chosen to avoid the city of Jerusalem, he might have evaded or at least postponed his suffering and death. Instead, at various point throughout his ministry, Luke reported that Jesus intentionally "set his face to go to Jerusalem" (See Lk 9:51; 13:22; 17:11; and 19:11). In this way, the inevitability of his death served as backdrop for his entire ministry.

Jesus' third and final prediction of his death and resurrection was recorded in Luke 18:31-34 (with parallel passages found in Mt 20:17-19 and Mk 10:32-34). In the Gospel of Luke, this story was positioned late in Jesus' public ministry, just prior to his entry into Jerusalem prior to his final celebration of Passover. When compared to the two previous predictions, this passage provided the most details about the events that will take place shortly. There was also a sense of urgency associated with this account. Again, Jesus took the disciples aside and spoke frankly. Rather than avoiding the city of Jerusalem, Jesus announced his intent to "go up" to the city. Referencing Scriptures describing the work of the Messiah, Jesus indicated that the prophetic writings would now be fulfilled. What would happen? In Luke's account of the prediction, "the Son of Man" would be handed over to the Gentiles, that is, the Roman government. This focus of the role of the Romans in the condemnation process was clearly contrasted with the accounts shared in Matthew and Mark. In these accounts, the Jewish religious leaders shared responsibility for the condemnation (Culpepper, 350-51). After painful physical abuse and humiliation at the hands of the

Gentiles, the Son of Man will be killed. Then, on the third day, he would rise again.

As was the case in the second prediction, the disciples once again did not comprehend the shocking information that Jesus had just shared with them. Furthermore, in both accounts, the disciples seemed to be blocked from understanding the content of the predictions. Some biblical scholars assume that God mysteriously hid the meaning of the prediction from the disciples. Others proposed that the news was simply beyond their present comprehension; they would only grasp the message after the predicted events had transpired. This second group of scholars paraphrase verse 34 as, "human intelligence could not grasp it; it had to come by revelation and experience" (Craddock, 216).

In the Gospel of Luke, Jesus clearly understood the consequences of this decision to declare his unique relationship with God and to claim his mission in life based on that relationship. He was ready and willing to suffer and die as a result of his commitment to God.

Exploring the Scripture: The Demands of Discipleship

Moreover, as reported in the Gospel of Luke, Jesus wanted each of his followers to unmistakably grasp the implications of his or her decision to follow him. In several stories recorded in the Gospel, Jesus described the demands of discipleship to those persons whom he had invited to follow him. In other passages, would-be disciples sought out Jesus. In both cases, Jesus shared surprising demands, paradoxical statements, and disturbing images designed to challenge his disciples and would-be disciples to carefully consider the consequences of their commitment to him and to his ministry. These stories illustrated the powerful truth that "The lot of the disciple can not be different from the lot of the one whom he follows" (Tolbert, 89).

This principle was perfectly exemplified in the complimentary texts, Luke 9:21-22 and Luke 9:23-27. In the former passage, previously described in this session, Jesus first predicted his own death and resurrection. Immediately following this prediction, in the latter passage, Jesus described several astonishing expectations that must characterize the life and attitude of his disciples. In short, he implied that, if the master must endure suffering, rejection, and death (as described in verses 21 and 22), then so must the disciple.

The seemingly impossible demands began with self-denial in favor of God's purposes. Frightening images of the cross, the Roman instrument of death, were also used to describe the daily and costly commitment of the disciple. If Jesus must die on a cross, then his disciples must learn to live with the cross. They must also be able to live into the paradox of giving up one's life in order to gain it. Finally, those persons who failed to completely identify with Jesus and his ministry now would experience shame and derision in the coming Kingdom of God. According to Jesus, these amazing and paradoxical behaviors and attitudes must be a part of the basic character of the people that Jesus had invited to be his disciples.

In Luke 9:57-62, the Gospel writer reported Jesus' responses to three different people who volunteered to become his followers. In each case, the would-be disciple expressed a condition for his commitment. Given the opportunity to practice "bait and switch" discipleship, to accept converts with conditions, Jesus resisted the temptation and offered challenging counsel.

According to Baptist scholar Malcolm Tolbert, the first man seemed unaware of the implications of his request to follow Jesus. Taken literally, when he said, "I will follow you wherever you go," (v.57 NRSV), he was not aware that, for all practical purposes, Jesus was a homeless person who would ultimately be killed by the Roman government. Could this would-be disciple accept having no place to lay his head? Would this potential convert be willing to follow Jesus to the cross?

The second man seemed to have a plausible reason to delay his promise to follow Jesus. Consistent with Jewish tradition, this man had a sacred obligation to take care of his father until the time of his death. Jesus responded to the situation by questioning conventional wisdom and practice. In paraphrase, he said, "Proclaiming the Kingdom of God must be your first priority. There can be no higher loyalty or responsibility, not even family obligations."

According to Tolbert, the situation described by the third man demonstrated a lack of decisiveness and commitment. He waffled between the comforts of home and family and the realities of discipleship. To the third man, Jesus said, "Make your decision and don't look back."(89)

In their encounters with Jesus, these would-be disciples learned that participation in the Kingdom of God required commitment without qualification, reservation, or regret.

The true cost of discipleship was also described in Luke 14:25-33. In this passage, the Gospel writer indicated that a large crowd of people was traveling with Jesus, that is, they were literally following him. Before they made a decision to follow him in discipleship, however, Jesus wanted to clarify his expectation. Unwilling to lure the unsuspecting into unconsidered commitments, he turned to this group of potential disciples and issued three disquieting challenges:

"Whoever does not hate both self and family cannot be my disciple" (See v.26). In the previous passage, one would-be disciple asked to delay his commitment in favor of family responsibilities. Jesus responded to that man in terms of establishing priorities. In this case, his response seemed harsher. Must we really hate our parents, siblings, spouses, and children? Does Christian discipleship require that we despise our own identify and personhood? How can we make sense out of this demand? Some scholars believed that Jesus used hyperbole, or gross exaggeration of a concept, in order to get the attention of hearers or to make a startling point, a point that they might otherwise choose to ignore. Other scholars attempted to more carefully define the word, "hate." The literal meaning of the term is not "to be angry with;" rather the word means "to turn away from" or "to detach oneself from." With this understanding of the word "hate," the passage may be once again explained in terms of the priorities of the disciple. Based on this view, two possible interpretations of the passage are offered. First, the demands of discipleship must take precedence over even the most sacred of human relationships (Culpepper, 292). Second, the demands of discipleship redefine all other human relationships (Craddock, 182).

"Whoever does not carry the cross cannot be my disciples" (See v.27). In the second and third predictions of Jesus' death and resurrection, it was clear that his closest followers, the disciples, did not anticipate the suffering and humiliation that Jesus was about to undergo. How could this crowd of would-be disciples expect that the person whom they considered to be Messiah was about to die on a cross? In this verse, Jesus felt compelled once again to foreshadow his destiny and to expose the "shameful" demands of commitment to him and to his purposes.

"Whoever does not give up all possessions cannot be my disciple" (See v.33). At a time when wealth was considered to be a sign of God's special blessing, this expectation of discipleship was also startling and unexpected. Did Jesus really intend for those would-be disciples, and for his contemporary disciples, to literally give up all possessions before becoming his followers? Was the phrase intended as hyperbole—a pithy saying designed to shock the individual or to explode conventional wisdom? Or was the saying offered as a prophetic vision of future events and re-defined priorities? Based on this third interpretative approach, the verse might be paraphrased, "Because Jesus faces martyrdom in Jerusalem, his followers must be prepared to leave everything behind and make their commitment to Jesus Christ as complete and all-consuming as Jesus' own devotion to his mission. (Culpepper, 292)

In addition to these three direct statements regarding the demands of discipleship, Jesus used three parabolic sayings to communicate his expectations. The first two sayings deal with the theme of "counting the cost." The third saying deals with the perseverance of the disciple.

In Luke 14:28-30, Jesus described a common task in the agrarian culture of that day: building a watchtower from which a landowner or farmer could inspect his fields and crops. Common sense dictated that the builder should plan the project and estimate its cost in advance. How embarrassing it would be to begin the project and be unable to finish it!

In Luke 14:31-32, Jesus told the story of a certain king who considered the cost of going to war against another king. What should be considered in the preparations? How do troop strengths match up? If failure is inevitable, would it not be better to negotiate for peace? In this case, the failure to plan could be not just public embarrassment but the difference in life and death.

Finally, in Luke 14:34-35, Jesus offered a third parabolic saying to summarize his understanding of the long-term implications of a decision to follow him. Basically, he asked the question, "Will your initial enthusiasm to follow me carry through, even in the face of unforeseen challenges?" The true disciple will answer "Yes" and will remain "salty;" the would-be follower whose commitment wanes over time is useless, just like salt that has lost its savor (Tolbert, 122).

In Luke 14:25-35, Jesus asked his potential followers, in that context and in the contemporary context, "Are you sure that you wish to follow me? Is the price more than you are willing to pay?"

The Cost of Contemporary Discipleship

In spite of the fact that "bait and switch" discipleship is often prevalent in the contemporary context, Jesus continues to demands costly discipleship from those who choose to be his followers. Part-time disciples need not apply. Partial commitments are not accepted. Because Jesus experienced the ultimate consequences of his decision to be the person that God called him to be and to do the ministry to which he was called, the contemporary disciple must be prepared to make the same decisions and to face similar consequences.

What is the cost of contemporary discipleship? Everything!

Resource Page

What is your reaction to the "bait and switch" approach to discipleship described in the introduction to his session?

_____

_____

_____

_____

_____

_____

Read Isaiah 52:13–53:12, the fourth Servant Poem. Describe the nature of the suffering and humiliation that the servant must endure. How may these images have informed Jesus's understanding of the consequences of his decision to indentify with the servant?

_____

_____

_____

_____

_____

_____

In Luke 9:37-45 and 18:31-34, Jesus plainly predicted his suffering, his death, and his resurrection; yet his followers were unable to comprehend the meaning of his prediction. How do you explain their lack of understanding?

_____

_____

_____

_____

_____

_____

In our contemporary context, what does it mean to "take up your cross daily and follow Jesus?"

_____

_____

_____

_____

_____

Describe a situation from your own life experience in which you did not follow through on your commitment to Jesus Christ because the consequences were undesirable.

_____

_____

_____

_____

_____

Describe a situation from your own life experience in which you chose to follow through on your commitment to Jesus Christ, even though the decision had unpleasant consequences. How was this experience different than that described in the previous question?

_____

_____

_____

_____

_____

10 Character Developed through Reflection on Experience

Focal Passage: Luke 24:13-35

Central Truth of this Session

Through theological reflection on life experience, the true disciple of Jesus Christ can experience meaning and hope, even in the face of life's most difficult circumstances.

A Year of Experiences?

A few years ago, I attended a meeting of pastors and other staff ministers hosted by our local Baptist association. During this gathering, one of the pastors loudly boasted that he had thirty-two years of experience in ministry, all served in the same church. One of the educators who served on staff with this pastor quietly turned to me and said, under his breath, "He really has one year of experiences repeated thirty-two times!" I have to admit that the two of us shared a subtle laugh at the expense of this well-meaning pastor. When the laugher subsided, however, I was sobered by the power of this off-the-cuff remark.

Looking first at my own ministry, and then at my own spiritual life, I began to consider the question, "What is the difference having between a lifetime of experience and having one year of experiences repeated many times?"

Thinking Theologically

I believe that one response to this question has to do with the human capacity to think. Put simply, people can reflect on their experiences in order to learn from them. To varying degrees, all humans have the capacity to critique our beliefs, our practices, and ourselves. Individually and collectively, we can acknowledge our strengths and build on our successes. We can also identify our short-comings and correct our mistakes. Most importantly, based on past experience, we can create in our minds a vision for a better future; then we can make specific plans to make that vision a reality. In this way, reflection on personal experiences becomes a vehicle through which we may improve the quality of our lives.

For persons of faith, the ability to reflect is often expressed in theological terms. In their book, *The Art of Theological Reflection*, Killen and de Beer defined and discussed what they called "theological reflection."

> Theologian reflection is the discipline of exploring individual and corporate experience in conversation with the wisdom of a religious heritage. The conversation is a genuine dialogue that seeks to hear from our own beliefs, actions, and perspectives, as well as those of the tradition. It respects the integrity of both. Theological reflection therefore may confirm, challenge, clarify, and expand how we understand our own experience and how we understand the religious tradition. The outcome is new truth and meaning for living. (Kinnen and deBeer, viii)

In a related book, *How to Think Theologically*, Stone and Duke described this same process in terms of "thinking theologically" about experience. They effectively argued that, if theology is defined as "faith seeking understanding," then *all Christians are theologians by virtue of our calling.* When we strive to understand what we believe about the Gospel and how we, as individuals and communities, can faithfully live out Gospel truth, then we are theologians (Stone and Duke, 1-10). They further proposed that all Christians should be encouraged to develop skills in thinking theologically. These skills include listening to the wisdom of life experience, questioning old answers and preconceptions, participating in conversation and dialogue about life and faith, and developing a sensitive and openness to the movement of the Spirit (vi-vii). Based on these assumptions, theological reflection on personal experience becomes a vehicle through which we not only improve the quality of our lives, but, in fact, find richer layers of meaning in our experiences, even our most painful experiences.

Living in a Thinking Community

A second factor may explain why one person has a lifetime of experience and another person has one year of experiences repeated many times. It is not enough for an individual to have the ability to "think theologically" about his or her own life experience. One must also have the good fortune of living within a Christian community that actively encourages and supports theological reflection.

What are the characteristics of this type of community? The atmosphere is open and hospitable. Testimonies are shared and celebrated. Conversations about life and faith are conducted in formal and informal contexts. Hard questions are encouraged. More mature and experienced members of the community model theological reflection in their relationships and conversations. And, in moments of personal and corporate crisis, individuals step forward, calming anxieties and reminding everyone of the ways in which past crises have been faced with faith. Together, the members of the community create a place and a space in which Gospel truth can be revealed and practiced (Roehlkepartain 61-63).

Exploring Biblical Truth: On the Road to Emmaus

The focal passage for this session provides one example of theological reflection in community. In this passage, found only in the Gospel of Luke, two disciples struggled to make some sense out of the recent events of their lives. When a stranger was able to reinterpret their experience, their despair and confusion were transformed into a heart-warming rebirth of hope.

In the walk to Emmaus, Luke 24:13-35, Luke painted a poignant story of grief and loss. On the Sunday after the crucifixion and burial of Jesus, "two of them" walked down the steep road from Jerusalem. Before the end of the day, they would walk approximately seven miles to a village identified as Emmaus. Scholars are uncertain of the exact location of this town. It was assumed that these two men were "disciples" of Jesus, a term that Luke used to designate a broad circle of friends and followers who would have had significant contact with Jesus during his ministry. One of these men was identified as Cleopas; the other was unnamed.

As the story unfolds, it was obvious that both of these travelers were deeply troubled by the events of the previous week, events to which they had presumably been eyewitnesses. To their understanding, they had witnessed the assassination of their friend, a murder supported by their own religious leaders and by the state. As they walked, they could talk of nothing else. At some point in their journey, a stranger approached them from behind, making his own descent from Jerusalem. Luke identified the stranger as Jesus, but the two disciples could not make that identification. Some scholars speculated that the two did not recognize Jesus because they were shocked and emotionally overwhelmed. Others followed a more traditional interpretation in which the two men were somehow miraculously blocked from identifying the stranger (Tolbert 184). In either case, the two men were not seeing clearly.

The stranger joined the two disciples on their journey and asked about their conversation. Immediately, the two stopped and looked sad. Cleopas eventually recovered enough composure to ask the question recorded in verse 18: "Are you the only stranger in Jerusalem who does not know the things that have taken place there in these days?" How do you understand the tone of this question? Was it asked in disbelieve and shock? Was it a gentle rebuke of this uninformed stranger? Or were these two so overwhelmed by the events of the past days that they simply expected the whole world to share their grief? Regardless of their attitude toward the question, when the stranger asked for more information, they shared their painful story.

The commentary recorded in verses 19-24 indicated that these two disciples had already begun to reflect on their time with Jesus and on the events of the past few days. After reading this portion of the passage, one is left with the impression that the two disciples were desperately trying to make some sense of these events, that is, to think theologically about their experience. It seemed, however, that they were having little success in the endeavor. Because they had been eyewitnesses to the public ministry of Jesus, they knew beyond all doubt that he was a mighty prophet of God and for God's people. But they had hoped for more. Based on their understanding of Scripture and their experiences with him, they had hoped that Jesus would also be the "one who would redeem Israel," a term loaded with theological and messianic significance. This part of the passage implied that they had not only lost a beloved friend; they had lost their vision for the restoration of their nation. In short, they had lost hope. In the second part of their commentary, hopelessness gave way to bewilderment as the two disciples described the rumors of an empty tomb that were circulating among their companions back in Jerusalem.

In verses 25-27, the two disciples received a lesson in theological reflection from an unexpected source. Suddenly, the uninformed stranger whom they met on their sad journey became what the commentators called the "unknown expositor"(185). The disciples were probably stunned by the tone of the stranger's response to their painful story. Expecting sympathy, the pair received a rebuke. The stranger called them "foolish" and "slow of heart." Expecting words of comfort, the duo received an extended tutorial in messianic theology. The stranger began his theology lesson by questioning the disciples' understanding of the nature and mission of Messiah. With these words, the disciples learned that, in processes of theological reflection, deeply held beliefs must sometimes be questioned and modified. In an attempt to offer the disciples a new frame of reference, the unknown expositor delivered an extended lecture in which he used the entirety of the Jewish Scriptures to reinterpret the life and ministry of the Messiah.

The Gospel account reported that, at the end of the day, the trio reached Emmaus. The stranger attempted to continue his journey, but the two disciples convinced him to stay and share their accommodations. At the appropriate time, they gathered for the evening meal. Most likely, they reclined around a low table. The stranger took a piece of bread, a staple served at every meal, said a blessing, and shared the bread with his fellow travelers. Then, three events occurred in rapid succession. First, the disciples' "eyes were opened." Second, they recognized that the stranger was actually Jesus. And third, Jesus immediately disappeared from their presence.

In that moment of community at the table, in the breaking of the bread, the disciples were totally transformed. Suddenly, things made sense! By the reaction reported in verse 32, we can see that the disciples had been emotionally moved by the way that the unknown expositor had explained his understanding of scripture. But recognition and transformation did not occur on the road. It happened at the dinner table! A common theme found in the book of Luke is table fellowship. As followers of Jesus, the disciples had probably been present for a least of few of these fellowship meals. So it is not surprising that, when their "eyes were opened," they were able to recognize Jesus in his familiar position, breaking bread at the table. In that moment of community, the words of the unknown expositor were literally embodied in their presence.

The final verses of the passage described their reaction to this event. Reflection and revelation led to action. Immediately, they got up and returned to Jerusalem. While the scriptures do not describe the return trip, one can assume that the two disciples had to walk or run uphill for seven miles, after dark, on a potentially dangerous road. Nonetheless, they returned to Jerusalem to find their friends and to share the good news. Their day had begun in hopelessness and confusion; it ended with the rebirth of hope and a transformed understanding of their personal experience with Jesus Christ.

A Lifetime of Experience?

This lesson began with a chuckle at the expense of an unnamed minister. When the laughter faded away, a serious question remained. "In terms of your relationship with Jesus Christ, do you have a lifetime of experience, or do you have one year of experiences repeated many times?" The experience of the two disciples on the road to Emmaus demonstrated that contemporary disciples of Jesus Christ are not doomed to recycling the experiences of the past in order to face the future. Instead, by "thinking theologically" about our life experiences in the context of an open and hospitable Christian community, all of our experiences, even our most painful experiences, can be transformed into a lifetime of rich and meaningful experience with Jesus Christ.

Resource Page

Define the term "thinking theologically about life."

_____
_____
_____
_____
_____

Write your response to the statement, "All Christians are theologians by virtue of our calling." Do you agree or disagree with the statement? Why or why not?

_____
_____
_____
_____
_____

The two disciples on the road to Emmaus were dealing with a tragic event in their lives. They had lost a dear friend in heartbreaking circumstances. Describe your understanding of their response to this loss.

_____

_____

_____

_____

_____

Reflecting on a major loss in your own experience, what was your initial response to this loss? At some point after experiencing this loss, were you able to "think theologically" about the experience in order to find comfort or make some sense of the experience?

_____

_____

_____

_____

_____

Prior to their conversation with the stranger of the road, the two disciples had an erroneous understanding of the theological concept, "one who would redeem Israel." Based on his experience and his understanding of the scripture, Jesus redefined this concept for the pair. Reflecting on your own experience, have you ever dramatically changed a deeply held theological position based on new personal experiences or a reinterpretation of scripture?

_____

_____

_____

_____

_____

Do you have a person or community in your life who challenges you to "think theologically" about your own experience? If so, describe how this person challenges you.

_____

_____

_____

_____

_____

Character Developed Through Reflection on Experience

Bibliography

Bowie, Walter Russell, et al. *The Gospel According to Luke*, Volume VIII in *The Interpreter's Bible*. George Arthur Buttrick, Commentary Editor. Nashville: Abingdon Press, 1952.

Covey, Stephen R. *The Seven Habits of Highly Effective People*. New York: Simon and Schuster, 1989.

Craddock, Fred. *Luke. Interpretation: A Bible Commentary for Teaching and Preaching*, ed. James Luther Mays. Louisville: Westminster/John Knox, 1990.

Culpepper, Allan. *Luke*. Volume IX of *The New Interpreter's Bible*. Leander E. Keck, Convenor and Senior New Testament Editor. Nashville: Abingdon Press, 1995.

Gilmour, S. MacLean. *The Gospel According to Luke*, Volume VIII in *The Interpreter's Bible*. George Arthur Buttrick, Commentary Editor. Nashville: Abingdon Press, 1952.

Heard, R. G. "The Old Gospel Prologues." JTS 6 (1995): 11.

Hinson, E. Glenn. *A Serious Call to a Contemplative Lifestyle, Revised Edition*. Macon GA: Smyth and Helwys Publishing, Inc. 1993.

Kinnen, Patricia O'Connell, and John deBeer. *The Art of Theological Reflection*. New York: Crossroads Publishing Company, 1995.

Miller, William A. *Your Golden Shadow: Discovering and Fulfilling Your Undeveloped Self*. San Francisco: HarperSanFrancisco, 1989.

Nelson, Roberta. "Parents as Resident Theologians." *Religious Education* 83/4 (Fall 1988): 492-493.

Nouwen, Henri J. M. *Life of the Beloved*. New York: The Crossroads Publishing Company, 1993.

Penick, Harvey with Bud Shrake. *Harvey Penick's Little Red Book: Lessons and Teachings from a Lifetime in Golf.* New York: Simon & Schuster, 1992.

Roehlkepartain, Eugene C. *The Teaching Church: Moving Christian Education to Center Stage.* Nashville: Abingdon Press, 1993.

Schroeder, David E. *Follow Me: The Master's Plan for Men.* Grand Rapids MI:Baker Publishing Group, 1992.

Stone, Howard W. and James O. Duke. *How to Think Theologically.* Minneapolis:Fortress Press, 1996.

Tolbert, Malcolm O. *Luke–John,* Volume 9 of *The Broadman Bible Commentary.* Clifton J.Allen, General Editor. Nashville: Broadman Press, 1970.

Wright, A. "The Gospel According to Luke" in *A Dictionary of Christ and the Gospels,* Volume II, James Hastings, Ed. New York: Charles Scribner's Sons, 1912.